Unlearned

// RECLAIMING THE DARING TRUTH OF BIBLICAL FEMININITY

CHELSEY MEAD

Scripture taken from The Voice™. Copyright © 2008 by Ecclesia Bible Society. Used by permission. All rights reserved.

Edited by Rachel Mallison

ISBN: 0692699198
ISBN-13: 978-0692699195 (Chelsey Mead)

Dedication

This journey is dedicated to the bold and beautiful women in my life who have challenged me to live unburdened by societal expectations. Mal, Hannah, Kayli, and Rachel—you are rock stars of a different kind, and this journey wouldn't have been complete without you. Thank you for inspiring me to dream big, speak truth, accept God's tangible grace, and for calling me on my junk in the most necessary of ways. This book is for you, and women like you, who aspire to live radically empowered by the Spirit.

Contents

Acknowledgments

Special recognition goes out to The UNEDITED Movement, an incredible community of women seeking grace in our over-edited world. Thank you for speaking truth and encouragement from the trenches, and for creating a space for women like me to share their stories of hope and healing.

A Note to You, the Reader

You are not the only Christian woman who wakes up ~~some~~ most days feeling like an absolute *mess*. Let that sink in deep before we begin. If you are anything like me, you probably have a lot of questions. Some in your heart about your place in this world, some in your head about this book you just picked up. So, what the heck is unlearning, and how do we do it? I am *so* glad you asked. Let's get to it.

UNLEARNING: [ˌʌnˈlɜːnɪŋ]
noun, the process of naming, owning up to, and dumping out all the junk we have learned about our identity as women from our culture, churches, and families.
verb, replacing that junk with the truth of God's Word and not a single thing more.

For starters, know that I am not an expert by any means—that is why I am the one writing the book. This journey is meant for the average, every-day woman. Whether you believe in Jesus Christ, or simply have questions about how He views women, there is room for your story, questions, and frustrations here. I mean that, truly. I have left plenty of room on the pages of this book for your story to be poured out and untangled, right next to mine. Plain and simple: I want you to make this thing your own.

I get it. I really do. Do we really need yet *another* book on Christian womanhood? Please allow me to yawn as I skim through the next 200 pages, right? Well. Maybe not.
I think it is time for a different kind of book.

I think it is time to say enough is *enough*.
I think it is time we cut through all the B.S. of what we have been taught about what it is really like to be a "good, Christian woman."
This journey can be many things for you, and it is not up to me to decide *exactly* what it will look like. What I can tell you, however, is what this book absolutely is *not*.
This is not a five step program to being a "better woman".
This is not a quick fix for your identity struggles.
This is not a lecture on throwing away your bikinis.
This is not a book about a perfect marriage meant to serve as some kind of ridiculous standard for you to measure up against.
This is not a book full of *"you should's"* and *"you are not's"*.
This is not a place of condemnation or judgment or flawless skin or perfect hair.
This book is my messy living room, still covered in last month's laundry.
This book is my face full of pimples and unwashed hair that's been covered in dry shampoo for the third day in a row.
This book is the two of us, sitting at a coffee shop in our sweatpants, throwing our hands up in the air because we just don't have it all figured out.
This book is my story, the unfiltered version, where I sit on the floor of my college dorm room convinced that God's grace is not enough for me.
This book is the beautiful moment of redemption, when Jesus rescued me out of darkness.
This book is meant to be a journey for all of us, the kind where we stumble and fall along the way, and learn to laugh at ourselves and trust that God really, truly, is for us as women.
As daughters.
As wives.
As mothers.
As sisters.
As friends.
As mentors.
As students.

As missionaries.
As world changers.
As all of the things that He designed for us to be—maybe some things we are not so used to hearing anymore.

The bottom line? I am not here to tell you how to live your life. That is not my job, nor is it my place. The truth is, I don't *actually* know you. I have no idea the specific nature of what you are walking through in your day to day life. What I do know is this: We all struggle in one way or another, and chances are, you have some questions about this illusive idea of biblical femininity.

So, I *am* here to talk about the kind of life you are free to live because of Who Jesus is and what He has done for you. I am here to tell you that you are absolutely not alone in your questions, frustrations, brokenness, or doubt. You are not the only one, Christian or not, who wonders why the heck it is so, dang hard to be a woman in this world. Hear and know this; We are all fighting the same battle. It may be on different grounds, but we are all certainly fighting nonetheless.

Surely you are tired from carrying the weight of this world and its expectations on your shoulders. Your hands must be bleeding, cracked, and sore from trying to hold it all together by now, and your legs ever-weary from treading water while you try not to drown in the chaos.

It is okay to admit that this being a woman business is damn well exhausting (yes, I said damn). We know the desperately overwhelmed feeling all too well. We have accepted it as "normal" and labeled ourselves as failures when we cannot bear its weight. I think it is high time for a new set of expectations, don't you?

So, if you have ever wondered...

- What is a woman's role in ministry? Is there a place for me?
- What about submitting to my husband? I am not sure I "get it."
- What about feminism? Am I even allowed to think that way?
- Why do I feel like pressured to look like a Victoria's Secret model? Ain't nobody got time for that, right?

This book might just be for you. Let this introduction serve as a challenge to where you stand today.

Do not pick this book up halfheartedly.
Do not expect the answers to come easily.
Do not start this journey if you are not willing to commit.

I tell you in earnest, unlearning is not for the faint of heart. This process is going to involve a little of me, a little of you, and a lot of God showing us where we need to experience growth. It is going to ask you some challenging questions; the messy kind we like to stay away from. It will dare you to live life in a way that radically impacts the women around you. We are going to reclaim the daring truth of biblical femininity.

Are you up for the challenge?
Good, I hoped you would be.

Welcome to unlearned--it is a safe place here, and you will not be judged. So grab your coffee and your baggage, it's time to go on a little adventure.

Introduction:

Chels, here. It all started at such a young age for me—questions about being a girl, what it meant to be a woman, what my role was as I journeyed further into our culture. For instance, when I was just five years old, I distinctly remember coming home in a fit of rage. Well, it was probably more like a temper tantrum, but for drama's sake—I will claim I was in an uproar. "Mom!" I yelled out, huffing and puffing as I ran into the living room, "My teacher told me that I have to change my last name when I get married and turn it into my husband's last name! That just seems unfair. Do I have to, mommy? Why can't I make *him* change *his* last name instead?"

My poor mother. She smiled. She even managed to laugh. Looking back, I am sure she was screaming inside, "Wait, what? She is barely *five*. What's she going to be like at 16?" *Spoiler alert:* Yes, I did get married and yes, I did change my last name. Don't worry, we will get to all of that later.

From a young age, apparently starting in kindergarten, I was always slightly irked at this idea of "Women's ministry," whatever *that* means. Was it tea parties and roses and purity rings and preparing yourself to be a wife? Was it something else entirely, and I just misunderstood what I was taught in Sunday School? Something told me there was more to this "being a Godly woman" stuff than wearing pantyhose and sitting still in the pew on Sunday morning. Somewhere in my heart, I knew that women held a special place in the world our God created. So why wouldn't anyone tell me where that place was, or how to get there? Why were we all content to sit by and have the same old conversations about submitting to our husbands, accept our roles as the weaker vessel, and not ask any questions?

Layer upon thick layer of bitterness and confusion built up in my heart until I found myself in a Women's and Gender studies class somewhere around the age of 18. I didn't completely agree with *everything* my blue-haired professor was spouting about being a woman, but you know what? It sounded a heck of a lot better than what I was hearing at Church.

I knew deep down that burning my bras would not solve the problem, I mean, those suckers are too expensive to replace, am I right? And picketing for equal rights, while I definitely considered it, somehow seemed as though it would wage war on the Church and their view of women. I was afraid to speak up in my Christian circles because feminism had become a four-letter word, and I was not about to be the first to drop that F-bomb. I surely wanted to do more than bake cookies for my neighbors and become a housewife—not that there is anything wrong with that, by the way, but I *desperately* wanted to know if I was allowed to have a choice in the matter. Was I even allowed to ask these questions? Would Jesus still love me if I turned into a feminist?

Somewhere between the limitations of feminism and the sometimes misguided, albeit good intentions of the Church, we can reclaim what it means to be a woman chasing after God's heart. Before we pick up anything new, however, we seriously have to get rid of the old. We have to purge our weary hearts from all of these unrealistic and unbiblical expectations. We have to rid our minds of false standards on both sides of this discussion. We have to make space for truth, and leave room for growth.

Get ready. It's about to get *real*.

I will do my best to be transparent on my part, starting now. I feel completely ill-equipped to write this thing. I am not an advanced scholar on biblical femininity by any stretch of the imagination. I am a fairly average college grad who is investing much of my time into unlearning all of the bad habits I was raised with as a product of our culture. My goal is not to bash where I came from, but I was certainly handed more Barbie dolls than GI joe's as a kid, and definitely had plenty of eyebrows shoot up at me when I joined the ROTC program instead of a sorority in college.

I am writing this because I, myself, still have plenty of unanswered questions. I am convinced that the majority of women in our society have deeply rooted, strongly ingrained lies wrapped around their hearts with a grip so tight that they are stifled in the way they view themselves. What's even scarier, I think we are *all* stifled in the view of who God made us to be as women—maybe even of God Himself.

This is what I want for us:
To know who the Lord says we are.
To understand His heart for using women in ministry and missions and doing great things around the world.
To see ourselves the way Jesus does.
To see our hearts, the way He created them—long before hurt, suffering, and doubt crept in like a thief to steal their joy.
To live our lives with all of the God-given potential played out in full force.
To kick shame and guilt into the pit of hell where they belong, so they can stop following us around like a dark cloud all the dang time.
To know His character more fully, His love more deeply, and to base our identities on that and that alone.

I have a feeling this is going to take some hard work. Speaking for myself, when I take a good, hard look at my life, I feel *pressure.* It is absolutely insane. Maybe you can relate. I am busy. I am tired. I never feel like I have enough sleep, yet I am awful at making time to rest. Hell—I am bad at making time to love my husband. I have been a wife for about ten minutes in the grand scheme of things and the thought of submitting to my husband, Taylor, seems both comfortable and terrifying all at the same time.

We found out we were expecting our first bundle of joy, Benaiah, halfway through this book writing process. The mere thought of figuring out motherhood in this day and age has me wanting to pack my bags and head for Africa all over again. I have many conflicting thoughts when I compare what I have learned about womanhood from an academic standpoint to what the Church has always taught me. There are two prize fighters in this femininity discussion, and both of them are losing as far as I am concerned. This world in all of its scholarly prestige does not have the answers that we are looking for. You know what? The Church alone does not have those answers, either.

We have become so caught up in trying to figure out what we are allowed to do, and wear and say, when we are allowed to do it, where we are allowed to wear it, and the politest way to say it, that we have made a Bermudan Triangle out of the entire femininity conversation—we may go into it with good intentions, but everyone just ends up lost and confused. So, where do we start?

We must find the root of the problem; the source of the weight we unnecessarily carry on these tired shoulders. It is time to name the very thing that started this whole mess, in order that we may rid ourselves of it entirely. This weight-baring load has a name, and that name is *guilt*.

If I had to take the overall emotional pulse of the women I know in my life, I think we would see a scary, but accurate, truth of how the demands of Christian womanhood have worked their way into our hearts. If I had to pick a single word to describe this pulse, the overall feeling towards ourselves and how we're doing in terms of being good, successful, Christian women, it would be guilty.

We feel guilty, don't we? We feel that we are emotional burdens to those around us. We believe that we demand too much of our husbands, friends, and families. We think that we cannot or will not live up to the ideals of wife and mother that the women in our lives have imparted to us. We sense that when we go to Church, we are not doing enough. We *genuinely* believe that these *other* women must have some secret formula for doing it all—respectful kids, the successful career, the perfect husband, *and* time to do their hair and keep up with their perfectly-styled Instagram feed. We believe that we must be missing something, and if we just pushed ourselves a little bit harder, God would "bless us" with whatever we feel we are missing. We would have it all and look *really* good doing it.

We think this way because we have not only misunderstood the scandal of grace—we have also failed to let it reign in our hearts. We have traded it in for the burden of guilt, and it is only going to get heavier the longer we carry it. The time we spend striving towards false standards of perfection reveals the very motivation behind our actions. If we are dragged along for the ride by our guilt, progress for progress' sake will never be enough. We will view ourselves as failures each time we do not meet another impossible goal. We will try and fail many times, out of our own strength, because we have it twisted in our minds that success, however we define it, is solely up to us.

You might be wondering, w*here did this guilt come from*? Can you even remember a time in your life without feeling trapped in its clutches? This is where we have to do the difficult work of separating the Christian-cultural definition of womanhood from the unhelpful guidelines enforced by our churches and society at large. The expectations from both are hurdles we were never meant to jump over. They lead to a damning cycle of striving, failing, feeling guilty for that failure, and it repeats on a maddening loop.

These expectations are like a carrot on a stick, both out of our reach yet constantly in our sight. They cause us to strive towards perfection with no care about the cost. So when we fail, as we all assuredly do, the guilt of that failure leads us to shame. We become ashamed of our efforts because they did not result in the perfection we were chasing. After the shame takes root in our hearts, it affects the way we think about ourselves. We have learned to talk to ourselves as though we are failures at our very core. As we will see later, when our thoughts change, so does our behavior. We will begin to act in the expectation that we will fail, and yet we strive for perfection and embrace the guilt all the same. Don't you think the cycle has continued for long enough?

In order to unlearn effectively, we have to own up to our junk— the perfection we chase, the guilt we hold on to, and the striving we have made into habit. It all has to go. This is going to be difficult, but it has to be done. We must acknowledge our flawed thinking before we seek to alter it. Then, surrender it to Jesus if we truly seek to rid ourselves of it. Finally, we will depend on Him to find our replacement for it.

There are two scriptures I want us to re-examine as we start this journey together. If you grew up in a church setting, you are likely quite familiar with them. If you did not, have no fear. Really. Get rid of it. We are going to look at them with fresh eyes and renewed sense of application. This time, it's personal.

"Create in me a clean heart, O God; restore within me a sense of being brand new." Psalm 51:10

Here, we see David pleading with the Lord for a change in spiritual circumstance. We can glean two things right off the bat from David's request:

- One, he felt that his heart was impure and dirty, and he wanted that junk *gone*.
- Two, he *desperately* wanted to be made new; to be restored, and he fully anticipated that he *would* be.

Sound familiar? It resonates with my weary heart, maybe it does for yours, too.

The word, *clean*, here in the original text actually declares a desire to be made pure, morally and ethically. It does not mean a literal cleanliness, but rather an internal restoration. This next phrase, *sense of being brand new*, is used to communicate an unshakeable certainty of being, granted by access to grace. David actually makes this plea after committing what scripture deems the worst of his offenses by turning away from the Lord. For our purposes, we can be sure that his words are full of desperation and longing for God to move on his behalf.

As we begin the process of unlearning, we need to keep this idea of restoration and attitude of desperation close. We can expect that our hearts *will* be restored into a new circumstance, and that God *will* move on our behalf. I don't know about you, but when I think of the sum of my experiences thus far and all that junk they've piled on, a new, *clean* heart sounds pretty fantastic right about now.

"Give up your gullible ways, *your naïve thoughts*, for true life. Set your course for understanding." Proverbs 9:6

The book of Proverbs, whether you have been a Christian for twenty years or twenty seconds or not at all, is full of instruction on seeking and obtaining wisdom. In this verse we see a command that I feel applies to seeking out these clean hearts and steadfast spirits. Here, we are told to set aside our naïve, old ways of thinking—to set our course for understanding. I love the language used here, that we must actively put aside our thoughts as we know they are prone to mislead us.

Secondly, we are told to set our course for understanding. The only reason we would need to set a course is if we were headed to a new destination, a new circumstance. So, let us do as we are instructed. Let us put aside our old ways of thinking. Let us unlearn them, and seek out our new circumstance as women, not burdened by the mandate of the Word—but empowered to do great things by it.

Consider this book your own personal dump zone—leave all the junk here and be rid of it for good. I want you to scribble in the margins. Highlight the heck out of the scriptures. Spill your coffee all over the pages. Fold down the edges of the things you want to revisit. Stain the hard parts with tears. Do whatever you like here, because this space is for you and this journey is all yours.

Questions for Unlearning

- What do you feel pressured to be as a Godly woman?

- What is the ideal you are trying to live up to?

- How have these pressures affected the way you view yourself?

- How have they affected your view of God?

- How has the guilt you feel lead to striving?

- What areas of your life are being dominated by this guilt?

- In what ways have you learned to expect failure, and in what ways do you treat yourself differently because of this?

- Where in your life do you see room for growth and renewed understanding of God's Word?

Initial Challenge

On a blank piece of paper, write out the first few things that come to mind when you think of the word, "guilty." What, specifically, do you still hold on to guilt over in your own life? What sins, habits, or negative thoughts are holding you back from accepting the clean slate offered to you by grace? Write them down, too.

Now we can reflect. Is this guilt you carry the result of a failure to turn away from that sin, or are you struggling to forgive yourself after Christ has already forgiven you?

Take a look at the scripture below. Read it through *several* times before taking another look at that paper you've scribbled on.

"The Eternal is compassionate and merciful. *When we cross all the lines,* He is patient *with us. When we struggle against Him,* He lovingly stays with us—*changing, convicting, prodding;* He will not constantly criticize, nor will He hold a grudge forever. *Thankfully,* God does not punish us for our sins and depravity as we deserve. *In His mercy, He tempers justice with peace. Measure* how high heaven is above the earth; God's *wide,* loving, kind heart is greater for those who revere Him. *You see,* God takes *all* our crimes—*our seemingly inexhaustible sins*—and removes them. As far as east is from the west, *He removes them* from us." Psalm 103:8-12

Hold your piece of paper next to this passage. Compare the two, side-by-side. Do you see the stark contrast? Which will you choose to believe—the truth of God's Word, or the guilt that seeks to warp your thinking? Today, you have the ability to accept free grace. There is nothing that prevents you from receiving it, and no lie of Satan that can lessen its power. You have the choice to either crumple up that paper and surrender those things to the Lord, fully, or to continue carrying these weighty chains. The decision is all yours, but my prayer is that we start this journey without the added weight. Let's ditch our heavy loads and get a move on, shall we?

Let us pray

Lord, we come before you today with empty hands and open hearts. We come to You, fully aware of our flaws and imperfections, knowing that we that we spent far too much time dwelling on them. We ask that this be more than just a book that we read passively in between life's many demands. We ask that you reveal to us the things in our hearts that were not included in your original design for us. We ask that you show us the burden of guilt we are needlessly carrying, and that you give us the ability to surrender it into your capable hands. We request that you untangle the lies from our weary hearts because if we were being honest, we would admit to you Lord, that we are so, incredibly weary. We ask that you take the away the sting of comparison as we are flooded with false standards of what it means to be a woman in this world. We ask that you give us a sense of being made new, and that our hearts are put under a new circumstance—one of freedom, healing, wholeness, and certainty in all that you promise to be on our behalf. Lord we come before you, repentant, of all the things we have tried to find our worth in that had nothing to do with you. We ask that you turn our hearts away from our striving and away from the lies of pursuing perfection. We admit that we are fully incapable of ascribing to ourselves our own worth, and that only You can truly satisfy. We release to you now our bitterness, our jealously, our anger, our moments of weakness. We give you all of the questions we have been harboring in our hearts about you. We surrender our doubt, anxiety, sorrow, and grief. We give every bit of it to you Lord, to do with it what you will. We believe in the authority you have given us as your daughters, and we boldly declare that this will be a season to unlearn the things you never intended our minds to dwell on. We ask that you set our minds on things above, things eternal, and use this time in mighty ways for your Kingdom.

Femininity 101

Before we get into this first topic, we will take a moment to pause and think about this idea of *femininity*. We can get our brains primed and ready for this conversation.

- What does it mean to you?
- What personality traits does it imply to you, specifically?

List 'em out here, and then we'll dig in.

-
-
-
-
-

Here's a quick bunny-trail on my background, since I actually feel somewhat qualified to write on the topics of psychology, sociology, and gender. I have always been fascinated with human behavior in the context of society, even from a young age. I mean, what twelve-year-old *doesn't* read the Diagnostic and Statistical Manual for Mental Disorders for fun, right? For those of you who didn't take PSYC 101 in college, that is the psychologist's version of the dictionary. Yes, I was the weird kid that read about schizophrenia and bipolar disorder while everyone else talked about their first boyfriends and texted on their Razr cell phones. I *did* eventually end up with a degree in Psychology with a few sprinkles of Sociology and Gender Studies thrown in. So this chapter will serve a basic, basic, (and one more time) basic overview of:

- How our culture influences us; and then later, we will dive into
- How we shape ourselves through habitual thinking.

This chapter will act as our guideline for working through the process of unlearning—and we can not really do that until we acknowledge what we know, and how we came to know it.

If it sounds a little odd, just go with me. It may get a little academic, but I think it might be beneficial. We need to have a mutual understanding of the ways we come to learn about gender, so this chapter will serve as the lens we use to view these issues surrounding femininity, and later, godly womanhood.

In a teeny tiny little nutshell, sex and gender are two very different things. Sex is nothing more than a labeling of your reproductive organs. Got ovaries? You're a woman. No uterus? You're a duderus. *I apologize in advance for any gender or sex related puns, I just can't help it.* Earlier, when I asked you about femininity, I was *really* asking you to describe behavioral traits that our society associated with being feminine. It is actually quite relative, depending on where you are and what you are doing. I did not ask what it means to be a *woman*, I asked what it meant to be *feminine*. Yes, there is a difference—and a rather important one. The words femininity and masculinity, obviously forms of the words masculine and feminine, do not describe *sex*—they describe *gender*. Gender is how we perform our cultural constructs assigned to a certain sex. Let's re-read that. Let's re-read that again. Got it? Well, just in case you don't, I will go in depth here a little more.

While your sex is ascribed as male or female at birth, your gender is a lifelong performance that operates on a continuum. We call this a social construct—something your society teaches you through very subtle but very real patterns of influence.

These influences may include your appearance, such as what clothes you wear and how you style your hair, but these influences are also largely behavioral. Depending on the environment, we act more in alignment with personality traits associated with being male, and at other times, we find ourselves all the way at the feminine end of the spectrum—champagne in hand at the nail salon, anyone? If you are skeptical, and you think I am off my rocker, read through these two scenarios and we will see if we can work through this together. Imagine the following:

Scenario One: You have a killer interview at one of the largest corporate (insert your dream job) offices downtown. You will be interviewing directly with the CEO, so you need to bring your A-game. Resume in hand and your best professional interview outfit on, you are ready to land the job. How do you conduct yourself in the interview?

Scenario Two: Picture yourself at a family reunion, with the side of your family you like best. It's okay—we all have one. Your little niece is running in the yard when she takes a tumble and scrapes her knee. She runs to you, teary-eyed, with a little scrape. How do you respond to your niece?

If you take a look at the first situation, I have some questions for you. Did you actively think about having a firm handshake when meeting the CEO? Did you think about negotiating a decent salary, or would you accept whatever they offered you? Did you envision yourself in a power-suit—or an outfit slightly "less girly" than what you may normally wear? Better yet, did you assume the CEO was a man? These are mostly traits that we associate with the masculine gender: assertive, strong, and proactively willing to negotiate for what they want, dominant of their environment.

Now we come to the second scenario. I am really hoping you acted differently towards your scraped-up niece than you did in the office with the CEO. That moment where you nurture an injured child is probably the epitome of what our society ascribes to femininity: nurturing, caretaker, reactive, gentle, and loving.

The difference in how you acted in the first scenario compared to the second? That is gender operating on a continuum. In neither situation did you stop being a woman, you simply and probably automatically adjusted the way you present yourself based on what you felt the situation required of you. There is nothing wrong with that, by the way, I just want to make you aware of how *easily* these gender stereotypes are reinforced, and how *deeply* ingrained they are in our society. So, you may be thinking, if we are not born with a gender, how does all of this come into the picture? When did I wake up and start acting female? How did I learn to do that towel-hair-flip thing, anyways?

This process of internalizing gender norms, what society expects of us based on sex and performed by gender, is called socialization. It is essentially the learning process by which we see how others act, male or female, and accept it as the true basis of our own behavior. This happens in two waves, called primary and secondary socialization.

Top Gender-Stereotyped Personality Traits:

Male
- Aggressive
- Active,
- Competitive
- Strong
- Courageous,
- Rough, hence dominant
- Reserved; emotionally distant
- Non-nurturing
- Logical, rational

Female
- Passive
- Noncompetitive
- Quiet
- Gentle
- Compliant, submissive
- Emotional, feelings are easily hurt
- Nurturing
- Illogical, irrational

It all starts with a gender-reveal party. If you are wondering, "Gee Chels, I thought you said that's called sex, not gender, so how can a baby have a gender before it's even born?" You are absolutely right. It is technically a sex-reveal, but I think somewhere in society, associating babies with even the word sex is somehow taboo, somehow inappropriate. I for one have not figured that out yet, so if you do, please send your answers my way. I digress...

...back to finding out the sex of the baby. The moment a mom and dad-to-be get the word, it is likely they will start planning an elaborate and appropriately documented "gender" reveal party. As I write this, Taylor and I are in the middle of planning our own sex reveal party for our little one. Blue fireworks on New Year's, anyone?

Take notice here, because you are a woman, I am assuming that you have been to one of these parties—see those gender norms at work, even now? Just in case you are unfamiliar with the concept, meaning you do not have a Pinterest account, let me set the scene for you. There is usually some kind of filled baked good, balloons, or confetti. Obviously, blue for a boy, and pink for a girl. At an appointed time, the couple will undoubtedly feed each other the cupcakes or cut open the box of balloons or in our case, light the fireworks. This then reveals the sex of the baby, and the showers of blue and pink begin.

This is where socialization begins. Before we are even out of the womb, mountains of pink and blue await us in our nurseries.

If you are still not so sure on all this socialization mumbo jumbo, I hear you. I get it. You might be thinking, *well, I was given plenty of choices as a kid. I was a tomboy, I was rough-and-tumble and my mom never forced me to wear ribbons in my hair.* First of all, I'm slightly jealous of your upbringing as I sported many huge pink bows throughout my lace-filled childhood, and secondly, you are in the vast minority here. Just think of the toys we buy for our little ones. When is the last time you bought a GI Joe doll for a girl? How about a play kitchen for a boy?

Believe it or not, our understanding gender performance really starts to set in during the toddler years. Think of young girls playing house, with little baby dolls in their strollers, or making dinner in their pretend kitchen. Any other Easy Bake Oven survivors out there? These activities all reinforce gender stereotypes.

Primary socialization is, just as it sounds, the *first* set of ways we learn about gender. This means, you guessed it, we mostly learn this first round of habits from our parents. This can either be healthy, neutral, or negative, depending on the environment you grew up in, but we will get to that just a little bit later. For now, let us focus on some examples to give you a clear picture of how much our little brains learn about gender long before adolescence.

Growing up, if you saw your mom, aunts, and other female relatives cook Thanksgiving dinner while the men watched football—you may have learned that cooking is a woman's job. If you saw dad mow the lawn, you may have learned to associate manual labor with the male persona. Alternatively, for those of you who grew up in a slightly more gender-neutral household, you may have seen the duties in the home more evenly divided. Regardless of the kind of gender norms you learned early on, the important thing is to recognize what they taught you as the basis for understanding this difference in roles for men and women. Do you agree with them? Do you find yourself still following some of the same familial scripts you saw in early childhood?

Most of the time, these behavioral-developmental milestones are seemingly harmless. It is a cultural foundation for understanding male versus female and allows our brains to make sense of the world around them, since the brain prefers to order things into various categories.

There are, however, additional issues we face which occur in secondary socialization. Oh, yes. There is a round two, and it has us ladies dazed and confused. This is about the time, if you are raised in a religious context, that ideas at church start to sink in and take hold. The adolescent years, when we are already suffering from daily identity crises at the hands of our hormones and acne, teach us the second set of rules about gender. This is where the ideas of what it means to be not only a woman, but a *Christian* woman, come into play. This is where significant damage can be done if we are not mindful. This is where we internalize gender concepts in religious contexts, thus creating our foundation for biblical femininity.

This secondary socialization? This is where we learn that ladies should be quiet, have a gentle spirit, dress modestly, and focus on preparing themselves to be homemakers. I get that it is not 1952, so sure, most of the time people will still ask what your college plans are and what ideas you have going on for your career. We have thankfully made vast strides in this department (though I *was* recently asked why I felt the need to "work outside of the home").

Regardless of where you are in life, there will always be an underlying assumption that you will fulfill the role of dutiful Christian woman defined by your community. For me, it was the ever-lingering question in the backs of the minds of those close to me, *"You do still want to settle down and have children, don't you?"* Have you ever thought about what this role looks like in your social-religious circles?

Gender constructs weigh heavily enough on our weary shoulders, but the mandate of Christian womanhood is an entirely different animal. It is one that we have to tame and re-train if we ever hope to live a life of true empowerment, and to impart better habits to the next generation of women.

So, you may wonder, what does the Bible have to do with socialization? Does it even address the issue at all? It absolutely does.

"Do not allow this world to mold you in its own image. Instead, be transformed *from the inside out* by renewing your mind. As a result, you will be able to discern what God wills and whatever God finds good, pleasing, and complete." Romans 12: 2

We are told in this well-known passage not to conform to the patterns of this world. We are instructed to seek transformation through the renewing of our minds. We are reminded that in order for our outward behavior to change, we must first change our thoughts. We can glean two truths from this passage regarding socialization:

- This is nothing new or unique to our generation. Societal pressure to conform to a predetermined standard has been around for a long time, and this pressure shows no signs of letting up any time soon.
- We can be comforted by admitting out loud that we are bombarded with some serious junk on a daily basis. It sucks. It really, truly does. But we are not left without a way to combat the chaos.

We are surrounded by ideals of what we should strive to be like.

The issue here is that most of these ideals don't come from scripture. They come from our Instagram feeds and people we don't even know at the gym. They come from advertisements and Pinterest and that negative voice we have running the show in our heads. It starts with society, yes, but this pressure quickly seeps into our thoughts and fights for control. This is why scripture urges us to *fight back*. This is why we are told our minds need transformation—not just a tune-up, but a complete overhaul of our thought life that bases its concept of truth on the Words of God Himself.

Do you see how this impacts your life yet? Are you starting to reflect? Can you think of the ways you have been taught to act, think, and portray yourself, because you are supposed to be a "good, Christian woman"?

Honestly, have you ever felt in some way inferior for not meeting the standards set for you by your church or Christian community? Do you feel empowered to love others in Jesus' name by these expectations, or are they more of a burden? Bottom line: do they lift you up, or weigh you down?

If you are feeling heavy, fret not. We are all with you in this exhaustion. We are all trudging onward in the same fight to reclaim truth. We are all taking labored step after labored step towards the Cross—towards healing, truth, and a renewing of our minds.

We are going to work through these habits and patterns one by one, until all that remains is the truth of God's Word.

Questions for Unlearning

- What have you equated with femininity?

- What are some of the confusions, myths, and expectations you have felt in your life as a Christian Woman?

- What did your family and upbringing, religious or not, teach you about womanhood?

- Do you view these ideas about femininity as positive goals worth working towards, or are they a burden?

Challenge: Two

Grab something to write *with*, and something to write *on*. Draw a line in the middle of your paper from top to bottom.

Think about the questions you just answered for a moment. What does your "good, Christian woman" ideal look like? (This can be answered using a real-life Christian role model, a mentor, or can be hypothetical if you don't have a specific picture in your mind).

Answer the following on the left side of the page:

- What are some characteristics you would use to describe them? Are they servant-hearted, humble, and patient?

- What fruit do you see coming from their salvation? Do you envision them having a Whole 30 Approved meal on the table by 6:00 every evening, with perfect hair and a clean house? Or, do they look like a missionary that hasn't showered in a few days as they trek through Southern Africa rescuing orphans?

- Below that, write about what you think their relationship with the Lord looks like. How would you describe their spiritual life?

Now, it gets personal. On the right side of the page, answer the following:

- What are some characteristics you would use to describe *yourself*? Are you stubborn, shy, or compassionate?

- What fruit do you see coming from your salvation?

- What does *your* relationship with the Lord look like?

- How would you describe your spiritual life?

- What's different about where you are today, and the ideal spiritual life you have pictured in your mind?

- What's stopping your walk with the Lord from looking like *that*?

- When you take a look at the characteristics you used to describe yourself and your ideal of Christian womanhood, did you use more negative language to describe yourself than you did your role model? Why or why not?

Here's the *real* challenge: What are some practical steps you can take, today, to make *more* of your relationship with God? If you're wanting to spend more time in the Word, what can you cut back on in your daily life to make space for this? (Lookin' at you, Instagram). If it is a renewed attitude of prayer that you seek, how can you actively increase your time talking to the Lord each day?

Whatever it is that you hope to change about your relationship with God, I pray you do so boldly and with a fierce commitment. However, please remember that *change takes time.* So be patient with yourself and make sure your goals are realistic--say it with me, *realistic,* to prevent any unnecessary future guilt from creeping into the picture. This time is all about progress, not perfection, got it?

Let Us Pray

Lord, we come to you in humility. We admit to you that we don't fully understand what it means to be a good woman in your eyes. We tell you truthfully that when we look at our own lives, we feel we are lacking, and we aren't sure why. We desire so strongly to leave behind all of our false standards of feminine perfection because what we really want to chase is *you*. We ask that you help us put aside the personal distractions in our lives that keep our focus from you, whatever they may be. We ask for your wisdom as we hold these unrealistic standards against the truth of your Word to see where our goals should come from. We believe that you can and will renew our views on womanhood as we surrender our cultural understandings in favor of an eternal mindset. We ask that you be our source of strength and perseverance as we set out on this journey. We depend on you fully to change our hearts, and we thank you for the work you've started in us.

Think, Think Again

Now that we are all caught up to this idea of socialization and how the Bible says we are to respond to cultural norms, let us take the next logical step in our unlearning process: It is time to address our thought life.

The Bible actually spends quite a bit of ink on our inner dialogue, and in the scriptures, repetition is key. In the original text, the authors did not have many ways to show emphasis. If something was important, it would be repeated. This is the way they communicated if something really, really, really mattered. They used *repetition* to emit *significance*. Since we see repeated verses on the consequences of our thought life, it must be important, right? It absolutely is. And we have years of biblical fact (and psychological research) to back that up.

Here are some verses to support this:

"It is the same with people. **A person full of goodness in his heart produces good things; a person with an evil reservoir in his heart pours out evil things. The heart overflows in the words a person speaks; your words reveal what is within your heart."** **Luke 6:45**

"Finally, brothers and sisters, fill your minds with *beauty and truth.* Meditate on whatever is honorable, whatever is right, whatever is pure, whatever is lovely, whatever is good, whatever is virtuous and praiseworthy." Philippians 4:8

"Stay focused on what is above, not on earthly things."
Colossians 3:2

Our thoughts are always going to reflect our heart towards any given matter, like a mirror. They tell us what is *really* going on inside. They are the first responders to the fight against our flesh. Shouldn't we be sure they are on our side?

Cognitive-Behavioral Psychology, my personal favorite, stems from one basic assumption: where there is an action or observable behavior, there is a thought pattern that preceded it. Simple, to the point, and right on the money—I think this theory is actually just a psychologically-framed way of the same verse we looked at earlier. Thus changing our thoughts becomes the biblically-directed starting point for us to begin the unlearning process. Our actions will not change until our thoughts do. Sound familiar? Romans, anyone?

If we can agree that our thoughts come before our behavior, we can recognize that they are truly, truly important in terms of identity. We will not expect others to treat us any better than we think we deserve to be treated. If we think we are junk, we will act like junk—and we won't flinch when someone else treats us as such. In the same light, if we think we are guilty of not being, doing, and striving enough towards the false ideals of womanhood, we will act guilty. We will feel needlessly ashamed. We will spend our days trying to dig ourselves out of a self-made hole. Something tells me this is not the thought life we are intended to have.

Let's step back and take a look at that phrase, the "thought pattern" that precedes our behavior. If these patterns are so important, what shapes them? What makes a pattern? And for our purposes of unlearning, how the heck do we change them? All of these are valid questions. Let's examine them together.

We call the relationship between our thoughts *associations*, but I like to think of them as multiple links that form a single chain, like a necklace. One idea leads to another, eventually looping back to the original thought, and so on. Then behavior is like the pendant—it is supported and carried by the links, or thoughts, on any given chain. (Did you catch how I just used a jewelry analogy here, because you are a woman and I am assuming it will resonate with you? Gender norms. They are *real*.)

Our habits, or repeated behaviors, are often preceded by similar lines of thinking over time. For example, if each day when you get dressed, you think about your appearance, body shape, and fitness level, these thoughts may lead to the behavior of exercising. In a similar context, the thought pattern that you are not "thin enough"—whatever *that* means, may have you reach for the celery instead of the chips at lunch time. These behaviors occur *after* well-established patterns of thought have worked their ways into your mind.

These ideas are very simple, but they can have huge implications for issues of substance, like our self-image. If we allow our thoughts to be shaped and molded by society's expectations for us as women, what kind of action do you assume that will lead to? If we are in the habit of thinking the way society thinks, we will continue to act the way society acts.

In practical terms for unlearning, we must recognize that our actions will not truly change until our thoughts do, and our thoughts will not change without the renewing of our minds through the washing of the water that is the Word. We are told in scripture to take every thought captive, to test and approve what is good. We must hold each thought in our hands, stare it down, and examine its origin.

Is this thought from the Lord, intended to spur me to make a wise choice?
Is this thought motivated by my flesh, prompting me to act out of selfishness, pride, or a sinful desire?

We must examine our thought life thoroughly because our flesh is constantly going to rail against us, seeking to alter our thoughts to align with the world we are surrounded with. Our flesh is like a sixteen year-old at prom—all it wants is to fit in, to blend into the social fabric, to look like everyone else.

The Word, however, as it changes us, *requires* that we look different. This is where we will wrestle, where the first battlefield lies. But, here is the good news: God's truth requires us to think on higher, eternal things. When we dwell on our Savior and what He has done for us—that is when we start to view ourselves in a different light. That is when our actions will reflect the change occurring in our hearts. When our thoughts are consumed less with self and more with Him, we can act, serve, and love accordingly. However, this process must start, and end, with Jesus. There is no other way.

So what can the impact of our thoughts look like in our lives, and in the lives of women around us? We can dig deep here and do some good by admitting the hard truths of how we view ourselves. The bottom line is that if we think we are unworthy of love, our actions and expectations will reflect that. If we believe we have less value because our bodies do not look like the ones we see in magazines, we have equated appearance with identity. If we believe we have no value without a husband, we have equated marriage with significance. If we believe we are failures, we will continue to fail. Any other acclaimed self-critics out there? Yeah, I'm talking to you (and me).

Even in all of this mess, we do not lose hope. Here is the *best* part: When we recognize the value we have in the eyes of Jesus, our behavior will change accordingly—because we will no longer be able to treat ourselves as if our lives are insignificant. Once we know and acknowledge our purpose, we must rise to meet it. As we focus our thoughts on who Jesus is, we will view ourselves in a new light. Our hearts will be transplanted into a new circumstance—that is, a circumstance of freedom from our negative thoughts. Of certainty in who we are because of Christ. Of compassion for others when our response is patience and not selfishness. Of joy as we allow our minds to be focused on how loved we *really* are. Of peace that cannot be stolen by worldly stressors. Of knowledge that we are valued far above the birds of the air and the lilies of the field. Our thoughts will change when we encounter Jesus—His presence demands that our thoughts dwell on Him.

"For though we walk in the world, we do not fight according to this world's rules of warfare. The weapons of the war we are fighting are not of this world but are powered by God and effective at tearing down the strongholds *erected against His truth.* We are demolishing arguments and ideas, every high-and-mighty philosophy that pits itself against the knowledge of *the one true* God. We are taking prisoners of every thought, *every emotion*, and subduing them into obedience to the Anointed One." 2nd Corinthians 10:3-5

So now we will take some space and spend some ink on this, too. We can boldly take the next step in our unlearning journey by answering this question: Where, in your life, do you see flawed patterns of thinking?

For me, those patterns have looked like many things. They have looked like guilt over mistakes in my past. They have looked like doubt in my creative, and even writing, abilities. They have looked like endless moments of comparing my life to those of women around me on social media. These patterns have resulted in many seasons of brokenness because my thoughts looked inward instead of upward.

You will hear more of my story as we push further, but for now, I want us to reflect. What are some of the unhealthy thought patterns you have playing on a loop in your mind? What lies are you grasping as identity? Is it that you are somehow unworthy of love—real, true, pursuant love? Is it that you are not good enough for whatever dream the Lord has instilled in you? Is it that you will never be free from an addiction? Is it that you will have a broken family that looks like the one you came stumbling out of? Is it that you will never find healing or forgiveness for the things you have done?

Whatever it is, get it out of your system here. Pour it all out so that we can call these thoughts what they are—lies meant to keep up cycling around the same broken message. We can address these thoughts head on, and find some biblical truth to replace them.

Questions for Unlearning:

- What patterns of thinking can you recognize in regards to your identity? What behaviors or attitudes towards yourself or others do they lead to?

- Are these patterns constructive and leading to actions that reflect a content heart, or are they destructive and leading to actions that reflect a life of striving towards false standards of perfection?

- If you could change your thought life, what negative self-talk would you get rid of? What would it look like if that negativity was out of the picture?

- What, specifically, do you need to ask the Lord to change about your thinking?

Challenge Three

This challenge requires a *little bit* of extra effort on your part. For the next twenty-four hours, I want you to focus on your thought life, specifically, your negative self-talk. Phrases that start with "I can't", "I won't", or "I am not" are typically good places to start. Keep track of them, either by writing them down in a journal, or making a note on your phone. Do whatever is easiest and will make you the most likely to record these thoughts.

Now, take a look at your list, and answer the following questions:

- What themes emerge from your negative self talk? Do they tend to be about appearance, worth, capabilities, or something else entirely?

- Were there certain times of day, activities, or people that accompanied them? (For example, did going to the gym each day evoke the thought, "I am not fit enough"?)

- Were any of these thoughts actually *true* or *factual,* or were they mostly based in opinion or comparison?

- Would you *believe* any of these things *about* a loved one?

- Would you *say* any of these things *to* a loved one?

- Why then, is it okay to speak to yourself in such a negative way?

You thought you were done, right? Not *quite*. It's time for the hard part. For the *next* twenty-four hours, I want you to actively replace these negative thoughts with something positive. You can do this by taking your list and countering each flawed thought with something that is *actually true*, and preferably based in scripture. Keep your list, containing the flawed thoughts and their biblical counterweights, handy. Each time a negative thought occurs, stop what you're doing (as soon as you are realistically able to) and read the truth of God's Word over that situation. Repeat it as many times as it takes for you to *believe* it.

I know, It might seem silly at first. To be fair, I *did* warn you this journey would take hard work, right? I promise you this: It is worth the time it takes to get into the habit of examining our thoughts critically. It is worth our time to view ourselves in light of who scripture says we are. Give it just twenty-four hours, and *see* what a difference changing your thought life can make.

"If you live your life animated by the flesh—*namely, your fallen, corrupt nature*—then your mind is focused on the matters of the flesh. But if you live your life animated by the Spirit—*namely, God's indwelling presence*—then your focus is on the work of the Spirit. A mind focused on the flesh is doomed to death, but a mind focused on the Spirit will find full life and complete peace." Romans 8:5-6

Let Us Pray

Lord, we come to you, exhausted. Tired. Frustrated. Broken. We confess to you that our thought life is far from what you intend it to be. We admit to ourselves that we spend much more time dwelling on our own perceived faults instead of resting in Your perfect love. We ask that you renew our minds, Lord. We know that Your Holy Spirit is the only true catalyst for change in our weary hearts and cluttered minds. We ask that you silence the noise. Drown out the distractions of our culture, so that all we hear is Your truth. Break the cycles of negative thinking that we're trapped in. Cut through the old habits and the current struggles. Teach us to take every thought captive, and to test them against your Word. Lord, let us not take our thoughts for granted and blindly accept them as true. Let us be discerning in spirit as we seek to pick apart the things we think about ourselves as a result of our thought life. Let us lift our eyes to You—and no longer live a life of looking inward to find answers to the questions rolling around in the backs of our minds. Let us dwell on Your character more constantly as we come to know you more fully. Change us, Lord. As only You can.

The F-Word

Feminism is *not* a threat to Christian womanhood, got it?

Feminism is simply a search for identity that is looking in some of the *wrong* places to achieve a few of the *right* goals. If you look at feminism on paper, which we are about to, you will see that its underlying principles and assumptions, are mostly good. The presentation is certainly attractive. It tells us that there is more to our lives than pretty looks and wifely duties. I cannot argue with that, and on most days, I will gladly celebrate it. I love the heart behind the feminist movement. I truly do. I am all for lady bosses and women doctors, equality of pay, and many other things that would never be viable options without the work done by our feminist predecessors.

The problem we face as Christian women is that most of us have not investigated any farther than the bra-burning and picketing for women's rights to see that feminism is not the bad guy. The enemy is still the enemy, and he will use anything he can, feminism included, to divide us against one another and distract us from the bigger issues.

Through a series of fortunate events, I ended up in an Intro to Women's & Gender Studies course during my sophomore year of college. Armed with an, "I-don't-need-a-man" attitude and an arsenal of tight dresses that I believed at the time to be empowering, I walked into a land mine of information that caught me—hook, line, and sinker.

Let me first address that there is, in fact, quite of bit of validity to the fundamentals of the feminist movement. Women do actually make only an average of .72 cents to every man's dollar. So-called "pink collar industries," largely staffed by women, tend to have lower paying salaries than those fields dominated by men. Don't believe me? How much does a teacher make compared to an electrical engineer? What about the fact that America is the only first-world country without paid maternity leave? What about the fact that after you have children, you will make an average of 30% less in your lifetime than if you chose to remain childless? *Ta-dah.* You have just been feminist-ed. That is the tricky part. Much of what is said and taught by the feminist movement is based in reality. Their solutions to these problems and their methods of seeking change are not always holistic in nature, but that does not mean they are inherently wrong about women playing an important role in society.

Let's be clear about this. Feminism was never intended to be about making choices for *all* women—it is about allowing all women *access* to the same opportunities (as men) *regardless* of their choices.

Want to have kids and still make a decent salary? Feminism.
Want to get paid maternity leave? Feminism.
Want to make the same pay for the same job done by a man?
Feminism.

Now, there are two important distinctions to make here that women largely get confused. There is a cultural definition of feminism, but that is *not* the same thing as the *definition* of *cultural feminism*. Maybe this has contributed to the misunderstanding of the feminist agenda, maybe it hasn't. Either way, as a young woman in this culture it is vitally important to know how to articulate your opinion for (or against) the feminist movement with grace and, well, facts.

The cultural understanding of feminism is an active, present fight for the advancement and improvement of Women's Rights—typically involving issues like the gender wage gap, second shift work, access to jobs, access to higher levels of education, access to equal opportunities after childbirth to include paid maternity leave, representation in the political realm, and several nods to reproductive rights. The definition of cultural feminism says something quite succinct and to the point, and defines a sub-category of the feminist movement (because yes, there are various types of feminism that fall along the feminist continuum from conservative to radical).

Cultural feminism claims that men and women do, in fact, have inherent differences, but that these essentially feminine traits should be valued and appreciated in the same ways that male attributes are appreciated; and that these values may be different, but are equally important to the overall functioning of society. In other words, we should be paid the same to do the same jobs, and should have equal access to those jobs to begin with.

Men and women are different, yes, but equal in value.
Does that sound familiar to anyone? I am convinced that cultural feminism is society's knock-off version of the way the Bible explains the roles of men and women. Don't worry, ladies. We have the real thing, and we have had it all along. We just didn't know it, and our churches refuse to see it.

My concern with feminist movement is that we have some well-educated, well-spoken women fighting for equality. For women. Who want equality. For women. Do you see the problem with this structure? If we claim to want equality, we better make it one heck of a fight. We have missed the forest for the trees, and now the woods are burning.

I have wrestled with questions about feminism for years.
Growing up in light of the third wave of feminist thought, I think

we, as women, are now under attack from all sides. What the founders of feminist thought intended to bring freedom of choice and equality of pay has turned into whiplash from the car wreck that is modern-day feminism. We are taught to want it all, criticized for trying to have it all, and stretched far, far too thin in the pursuit of the ideals of our society. We must put both career and family first in this game that no one wins. It is the ultimate catch-22, this feminist stuff.

Pursue a career? Have a family? Have both? No matter what you choose, as society has finally agreed that we have a choice, as if it were ever theirs to dictate, you will be questioned. If you're a stay-at-home mom, which we say with such a negative connotation by the way, why don't you want more? If you are a working woman—don't you feel empty without a family to fulfill your maternal instincts? Oh, you want a career *and* a family? Be ready for a smaller paycheck, criticism for taking your kid to daycare, and the relentless mom guilt at the end of every day that says *you are not enough.*

Stop right here for just a moment to remind yourself of some truth: We cannot be everything, to everyone, 100% of the time.

I will shout this from the rooftops until I am blue in the face. We are faced with some very sticky situations as women who live or breathe or work or have children or do all of the above. When it comes to appeasing societies unrealistic expectations for our lives, we cannot win. We are all caught up like runners on a treadmill. Sure, we work hard, but are we actually getting anywhere? Like a toddler trying to force a square block into a round-shaped hole, our solutions are not going to fit, because we are approaching the problems wrong way.

My issue with feminism is that it is, in a word, *limited.* Our argument should not *only* be to fight for equality for women. I believe we are in the right battle in our desire for advancement, but we are missing out on the majority of the war. We are thinking too *small*. Knee-deep in the trenches of feminist thought, we are so engulfed in the 72 cents we make for every man's dollar, that we have sincerely missed the point of equality. By picketing for Women's Rights, we have missed the opportunity to make advancements for human rights. We have squelched the opportunity to fight for humankind because we want to make sure our kids will not cost us our careers, and vice-versa. We are so busy criticizing the choices of other women and blaming men for our problems that the enemy has snuck in—undetected and unopposed.

The enemy has used feminism to shift our focus. What should be a spotlight on the injustice against humankind is now a laser pointer showing us a very limited, narrow view of the breadth of inequality against women in our small corner of the world.

We sit in a privileged country, rightfully upset that we are still deemed less valuable than men in similar roles. I think we can allow for this frustration, but only if and when we can step back to see the bigger picture. Only if this frustration for our own situation is matched by blatant outrage at the situations of others less fortunate. We may scoff at our thirty percent lesser paychecks, but only if we are willing to step up to the plate for women who are not taught to read. For men and women who are sold as sex slaves because they were lured in by false promises of employment. For young girls who are sold willingly like property by their mothers to pay off the debt of being born a woman. For women whose word is only worth one third of a man's in a court of law. For women who cannot own property or hold a proper job or finish their education because it is deemed a waste of resources. For men who are raped in the sexually charged subculture of our prisons. For young boys who are encouraged to turn to violence as a response to social problems instead of using their words. For men who are too ashamed to seek help for mental illnesses like depression. For men who are afraid of the stigma of being called a victim, so they, too, sit silently in patterns of abuse, unwilling to reach out because they fear that no one will believe them.

Reality check? The waves of feminism do not hold a candle to the equality of grace that Jesus calls us to fight for. What feminism, in its very existence, reveals to us is the innate and irremovable understanding that *something is not quite right.*

Feminist thought, widely successful in secular circles, is *evidence* that we were all created with an inseparable desire for justice and equality. Let me ask, Who do you think designed our hearts to crave such justice in the first place? Could it be that feminism comes from the remnants of longing for balance and shalom in our hearts, placed there by our Creator?

Feminism may give some flawed answers to the question of identity, but that does not mean all of its answers are inherently bad. They are simply incomplete because they are often unpaired with biblical truth. But when they are, what we see is a powerful and daring challenge to the overall treatment of humankind.

Where feminism says equal pay and equal rights for women, grace says equal forgiveness for all who have sinned. Unlimited second chances for all who have made mistakes. Unrestricted access to Jesus Christ for all the world...regardless of gender, regardless of race, regardless of income, regardless of your past. If we treated others with grace, in the ways Jesus calls us to, we have no need for feminism—because we would all be treated as equals from the get-go. Sadly, this is not our reality.

What we see is this: Feminism has simply stepped in where the Church has stepped out—afraid to make bold statements about equality because we are afraid of offending, afraid to join the messy fight and get our hands dirty.

So now we are left with a one-sided conversation on feminism, with the voices of believers sadly and obviously absent. We now live in a culture that believes progress is equally degrading both men *and* women. Instead of respecting women as people-not-objects, we have learned to objectify men, too. Instead of fighting a rape culture where women do not feel safe walking to their cars at night, we have created a cone of silence for victims male and female alike. Instead of making daring claims about the value of all life, we pick and choose who is worth more and less based on trivial factors. If where we are today is the definition of progress, I do not like where we are headed.

Efforts towards equality apart from Jesus and His grace are lost on us in terms of eternity. At the end of our lives, there is only one factor that will discriminate us from one another. It is not race, level of income, sex, marital status, education level, or any other earthly attribute we can come up with. It is salvation and salvation alone that will determine the course of our hearts. Our goal should be to fight for *that* equality--the kind where all have access to and knowledge of Jesus Christ. When people truly understand who Jesus is, odds are, the equality we are so desperately seeking will follow. For women. For refugees. For the illiterate. For the oppressed. For the enslaved. For the lost. For the unreached. For the forgotten. For the homeless. For the rich...

...because Jesus demands that we love each other in such a way that there is no room for discrimination.

We surely have a long, long way to go, but here is the good news: The equality movement of the Cross is much more daring, much more progressive than anything we have going on in our legislation. It is audacious, even scandalous, and so, incredibly radical that people still die for the sake of its advancement. It has the answers that feminism and post-modernism simply cannot give. It has truth and validation that no paycheck or career milestone can bring. It is so much *bigger* than feminism, and it has been around for over two thousand years—still going strong. The movement of grace can, and should, always captivate our hearts far beyond any earthly wisdom.

When I think of feminism in a scriptural context, as I often do, right? I am hit with some truth that can be difficult for even me to digest. Women in Jesus' day were not treated like property, they *were* actual property. They could not leave the home unaccompanied or without permission. They could not be religious leaders. They could not testify in court. They could not do a lot of things, actually.

Stories like Esther's and Rahab's in the Old Testament? They are not seen in quite the same radical context as we are about to examine because in the Old Testament, Jewish women were considered nearly equal to their male counterparts. We actually see a regression in the treatment of women as we approach Jesus' time on earth. His views towards us women folk? They are really quite extremist. Can you believe that? Right there, in the middle of the New Testament, Jesus is debunking the social norms to reach women. These are things that today, we would consider, well...feminist in nature—*if the Church allowed us to, that is.*

So, what kind of society were our Marys and Marthas living in? Well, they could not go to the temple, could not read or study the Bible, could not do many things we take for granted today. They were essentially slaves; second class citizens, even in the religious contexts.

This is the part where I do a double-take at the scriptures, because what I am seeing with my eyes seems too radical, too daring, and too extreme. I mean, have you *seen* how Jesus treats women in His days walking the Earth? It is unthinkable. More than just socially unacceptable, it is frowned upon by all the uppity ups and religious leaders of the time.

When Jesus heals the woman with the issue of blood in the Gospels, some incredible truth of His character is revealed. Not only do we see Jesus' sovereignty over the physical illness of this woman, we see Jesus make a daring claim for the use of women in His ministry. The woman with no name? That in and of itself is significant. Her name is not mentioned once in any account of this story. Why? *Because, that is how little importance women had in that day to the men who recorded it.*

She was unclean, terminally ill, and crawling around on the dirty street trying to sneak a grab at Jesus' robe. In the context of the New Testament? She was ratchet, y'all. She was dirty and unnecessary in every way, until Jesus recognizes her. She then becomes very important to us. Why? Because she was sick. Incurable. Unclean. It made you unclean to even be in her presence. According to the laws we see in the Old Testament, it should have made Jesus Himself unclean to touch her. That is how *drastically* wrong this picture looked to all those who witnessed it. That is how extreme Jesus was then and is now in the use of women for His ministry. Yeah, yeah. Your feathers are ruffled. Just let me finish the story, alright?

Spoiler alert: Jesus heals the woman and goes on to the next miracle.

But wait—if you breezed past the moment of healing, as I did for years, you will miss the most important part of the story. It is not *only* that Jesus heals her. We see time and time again that He can heal. That is not the only miracle, here.

We see Jesus do two things that probably stopped the disciples in their tracks. For one, that other healing Jesus is on His way to is for the daughter of a religious and political leader. This very important man of society is waiting on Jesus, as He stops to address this filthy woman that is grabbing at His robe. I bet you can imagine that man's impatience as Jesus proceeded to talk with the unclean woman. Oh, the audacity. The boldness. The blatant way that Jesus stops the story to hear hers in its entirety. Did you ever grasp that? Mark tells us that the woman recounted her whole story to Jesus. She has been suffering from doctor to doctor for twelve years, so my best guess is that this was no quick tale, but Jesus is not swayed or rushed by the pressures of society urging Him onward. He has all the time in the world to hear her speak.

Secondly, as she recounts her pain and sorrow, Jesus does something that we only seen *one time* in the entire New Testament. This moment? It is truly one of a kind. This is the only time it happens, ever. He looks to this woman...this outcast...and He calls her His *daughter.*

This is astounding. The woman that the apostles in all of their writing skills did not take the time to learn her name? Jesus calls her daughter. He hears of her suffering, removes it, and gives her a treasured, valued identity. What society deemed impossible for her circumstance, Jesus did in a single word. Can you see the moment impact her, in her lowly state? Have you felt that moment—when Jesus came to you in yours? The same radical Jesus that empowered her to healing and a valid identity is empowering us today.

He cares about our story, about our place in this world. He seeks to validate our identity—in fact, He is the only one who can.

But wait, there's more.

We cannot talk about radical grace without addressing the woman at the well. I have recently learned to love this story, too. Oh, how my heart—my sinful and redeemed heart, loves to hear this story. Did you ever stop to recognize the significance and beauty of this moment in history?

To set the scene, know that Jews and Samaritans were *not* friends. The place where they lived was called Samaria, and Jews avoided going there at all costs. If they needed to travel, they took a physically longer and more grueling route just to stay away the very grounds inhabited by the people they deemed unclean. *That* is how extreme their dislike for each other was. Really. So, when we hear of Jesus ministering to a Samaritan adulteress, we have to view that in the scope of this radical context.

Here, we see intentionality come into full play. In Jesus' days on the earth, Jewish men did not *accidentally* cross paths with Samaritans at all, but especially not Samaritan *women*. Given that a water well, a common place for community and fellowship, was typically a meeting place for women, it is odd to see even a Samaritan man on the scene. But, to see a Jew? To see Jesus, their already-controversial leader? That is something unthinkable and unexpected—and you can bet that Jesus did it on purpose. This adulteress...this, gentile....she is the *first* lady non-Jew that Jesus directly ministers to. Wait. Can I repeat that and get some "amen-s"?

This woman is the *last person* that Jesus should have been seen ministering to directly—as she is an adulteress living what we would deem a filthy life. Do you see this impact this has? Do you see how important this is? Jesus does not do these things by mistake. She's a *mess*; an unclean, sinning, Samaritan lady who's gone through a *few* different husbands. All the other woman scoffed at her, rolled their eyes at her. Translation: They did not like her Instagram photos and they did not respond to her text messages. This chick might as well have been the original "Bye, Felicia." She spent her days isolated and without community. Maybe she even sought the attention of these additional men because she had one of those awful longings in her heart that she thought could never be filled, until she met Jesus. Then, He speaks to her in the most public of public social spaces. Y'all. Jesus friended this girl on Facebook *and* wrote on her wall, got it?

There was no hiding His conversation with the woman—who, again, we are not given a name for because that is how little significance she had at that time. Jesus steps into a place of public declaration here. We see His heart for redeeming women, even the most broken and societally outcast women.

He publicly calls her on her stuff, don't get this picture wrong. He tells her like it is. But then He confronts her with the same extreme grace we are both rescued by and called to fight for. He tells her that the hole in her heart she has tried to fill with men can be filled with nothing but belief in His sovereignty. And we are just hitting the tip of this biblical iceberg.

What happens next? She goes and tells people about Jesus. Maybe you have missed this if you casually read this story, as I have for years, but this is the final picture: She becomes a missionary and she goes on to tell the other Samaritans about Jesus. This is unreal! This is *radical*. The woman-around-town encounters Jesus Christ in the flesh and becomes the first woman missionary that we hear of in the New Testament. He sends *her* out to tell others the truth of radical grace. So don't you tell me that there's no place for bold women in the ministry of Jesus.

To that end, let us quickly and with finality, address the issue of empowerment. The original use of the word refers to being made strong by the Lord. We are encouraged in the second book of Timothy to be *empowered* by grace, and we are told in Romans 7 to live a life *empowered* by the Spirit; not burdened by the law. It has *nothing* to do with taking your clothes off for money because it makes you feel good, as our society may have young women believe. FYI: That is not empowerment--that is exploitation. The two are polar opposites.

Since we have made a mess of this word, we can do some damage control, here. We can clear this up once and for all, so that our children and their children will not misunderstand the vital role they play. The world they are inheriting from us is a scary one. Let us teach them to cling to the ultimate road map of God's Word as they'll be navigating some choppy waters.

Empowerment is Not:

- Gaining the attention or approval from your male peers
- Limited to terms of worldly success (i.e. a job promotion, academic achievement, etc—though these are wonderful things, they do not define or attribute power for our purposes)
- Higher heels and a bigger paycheck
- Engaging in degrading sexual activity

Empowerment Is:

- Recognizing and accepting your true, unshakeable worth in Christ
- Acting and speaking with all authority granted to you by the Holy Spirit as a Co-heir with Christ
- Understanding your vital role in the advancement of radical grace
- Influencing other women to rise to the challenge of true godly womanhood

Let's keep working the "women are significant" angle for a moment, shall we? Let's talk about Mary. You know, Jesus' follower, Mary. To add to the picture of how women were viewed here, keep in mind that women were not seen as credible witnesses. In fact, if enough men said that a woman did something, she was guilty by their word alone. As for a woman, her testimony meant almost nothing. They were seen as prone to gossip and stories and had no place in important matters. If you had something important to say, you said it to a man. This is the societal norm, but what we are about to see is Jesus, yet again, turning this upside down and rewriting the script.

Think back to the resurrection—the foundation of our salvation, the holy moment of victory in scripture when Jesus is triumphant over death and hell and the enemy. This is the beautiful moment that has come to base our identity and our worth and our foundation for the meaning of life itself. This moment in history was first revealed to...a woman, Mary, specifically.

Why would Jesus, in His risen glory, choose to reveal His resurrection to a mere, gossipy woman? We *must* have significance in His story. Our value to society shifted in this moment when the greatest story ever told was first put into the mouth of a woman. Can you grasp the holy purpose for your life yet? Do you see the kind of true empowerment bought for you on the Cross? It is worlds better than whatever our society tells us is "power," because He gives us the power to bear witness to the work He has done in our lives.

Do you see what Jesus is repeatedly demonstrating here? Society tells women they are useless, worthless property, prone to gossip and nothing else. They were created to bear children and tend to the home—but not a single thing more. Their word couldn't be trusted. They weren't "in" on all the major decisions in their families, even the ones concerning them. They were second-rate, overlooked citizens with no rights. They were essentially indentured servants. But Jesus says they are, and we are, more.

Jesus shows us that regardless of how society views women, He came to minister to us, too. He gives us a place in His ministry, too. He shows us *our* word has validity because of *His* Word. He demonstrates to us that our life has meaning by revealing the resurrection to us, intentionally. He does so by using women to further the Gospel in a day when women couldn't even speak in a temple or hold their own religious opinions. We have a place, a huge place, in ministry. We always have. We always will.

Maybe feminism is just ascribing the afterthoughts of the way Jesus lived His life on Earth. The key difference in His ministry and where feminism is now? Male or female, rich or poor, Jew or gentile, Jesus is in the business of loving the outcasts, regardless of the societal norms. His ministry takes our ideals of feminism, and challenges us to go even farther by the empowerment of grace that calls us out of darkness. His ministry is one of equality, as we are all equally sinners with equal access to redemption by the work done for us on the Cross. He is the ultimate equal rights advocate, and we are called to pick up crosses of our own, and boldly follow Him.

I pray daily for the mind of the little boy growing in my tummy, and for the minds of the upcoming generation. In the midst of the joy, I'm already met with intense fear. I don't want our sons and daughters to grow up in a world that teaches empowerment to mean overtly sexual. I don't want them to grow up in a culture that claims men and women can do whatever they want to with their bodies, because in all reality, we can't and we're not supposed to. I do not want to see them confuse freedom of choice with a mandate of casual sex. I pray they never buy into the idea that it is okay to be bought—that their sexuality, or any other part of them, is ever for sale.

I do not want the up and coming women to grow up with a mentality of fear, where they shy away from making eye contact with the men they pass in the streets. Where they learn to pretend to talk on the phone if someone looks at them too long or not long enough—whatever causes suspicion in their paranoid minds. To always feel threatened when a man approaches, because, who knows what he might do. To both live in fear of men and in fear of not gaining their approval and in the fear of wanting it in the first place.

Yes. We must restore this idea of empowerment, and raise of a generation of men *and* women who are not afraid to rise to the occasion.

Questions for Unlearning

- What do I define as feminism?

- Do I tend to align with these beliefs? Why or why not?

- How do I view Jesus' heart towards women in the radical context of the scriptures?

- How does this change my view of women and ministry and our overall roles in society?

- Am I willing to accept the holy mandate for my life as a believer first, and a woman second?

- If I could change one thing about how women are treat in society, what would it be?

- What steps can I take in my thoughts and therefore actions towards making this a reality in my circle of influence?

- What do I define as a successful woman? And what is this definition based on?

- Do I feel in any way convicted to change this definition as I look at my own life?

Challenge Four

For this challenge, I will simply ask you to keep your eyes open.

Okay, okay. It isn't *really* quite that simple.
What I want for us regarding this topic of radical grace is to *look* for opportunities to *share* it with others. As you go into your daily routine, I want you to seek out ways to love the outcast, mistreated, or overlooked people that you encounter. It can be something small, like listening to the opinion of a co-worker who everyone typically blows off. It can be making polite, love-demonstrating small talk with the mom of a special needs child at the grocery store, instead of gawking at the challenge it is for her to run her weekly errands. Maybe for you, it starts with adjusting your thinking so that you *see* opportunities to show grace before you work up to acting on them.

Wherever you begin, my encouragement to you is this: do not underestimate the power of a small gesture done with great love. Sometimes the boldest statements about equality for humankind are actually little, beautiful moments where *one person* took the time to stop, look someone in the eyes, and love them in a way that says, "I see you. I hear you. I value you."

Let Us Pray

Lord, we thank you for the example of radical grace you have given us in the sacrifice of the Cross. We are endlessly humbled by the act of love you demonstrated by laying down your life for us, even in our sin and filth. We ask that as we seek to understand your heart for justice, that you would keep us mindful that we are all sinners in desperate need of you. We ask that you keep our focus on treating others with love in a way that dignifies them, and that we would not be so foolish as to fall into the trap of taking pride in our efforts to work for equality. We recognize that anything we do apart from your love is meaningless, and that our efforts apart from you are meager and without fruit. We ask that you make it clear to us the times and ways you want us to step out in faith to fight for justice, and that you would give us the boldness to do so. When we open our mouths to speak, we believe you will give us words to say, just as you did Moses in his fight to free his people. We know that you are a gracious Father, set on loving His children radically and without discrimination based on trivial factors. We ask that you teach us to love like you, and that it would advance your Kingdom on this earth in mighty ways.

The Modesty Myth

My guess? You might be dreading this chapter already. Honestly? So am I. Apparently I am not supposed to write a book to Christian women without talking about modesty. So, here we are, awkwardly twiddling our thumbs, pretending that we actually *want* to have this conversation. Another dang woman's opinion on modesty? *I already know what you have to say,* you might think. *Don't dress in a way that causes my brothers to stumble. Don't wear anything I'd be embarrassed to be seen in by my pastor. Always make sure my shorts are longer than my fingertips. Don't show too much (or any) cleavage because that will attract unwanted (potentially dangerous) attention. Don't ask for trouble.*

I have a five-word response to that, friend: What a load of crap.

What is the first thing you think of when you hear the word, "modesty"? Did you cringe? I know I just did. My mind instantly goes to that pair of leggings sitting in my closet, or the low-cut blouse I look maybe-too-good in. I'll tell you, I don't think of words like "beauty" when someone brings up modesty. My mind usually jumps to all the ways I fail in that area. I can instantly picture all of the things in my closet I probably need to go throw away and replace with turtlenecks. Am I the only one who feels this way? I highly doubt it.

Modesty, as I have understood it for most of my life, elicits the response, "I need to change something about myself." A completely healthy view on the issue, right? *Right.*

It all started with a phrase that got thrown around quite a bit when I was in the lovely and confusing and mostly awful stage we call being a pre-teen. It went a little something like this, "modest is hottest."

Catchy and easy to remember, this phrase spread like wildfire in all the youth groups. Young girls now had a seemingly solid refute to the world around them that had just entered the "show-off-your-belly-button" phase of teen fashion. Women and young girls alike were now taught that in order to really, I mean really, get a guy's attention—cover it all up. Leave some mystery for him to wonder about. Um, *gross*?

Let me see if I've got this straight. Not only are we told explicitly to be ashamed of our bodies, we are also taught that the end-all-be-all goal of whatever we wear should be to gain the attention and approval of a man? And it does not stop there. We should let his imagination run wild about what's underneath that "I heart Jesus" t-shirt that's two sizes too big, right?

What twelve year old needs to hear this?
What 30 year old needs to lug *this* baggage around as the basis for her understanding on modesty?

Modest is not hottest.
It's not supposed to be.
That's not even the point.

This very chapter is what sparked this entire book. I saw a body-shaming entry on modesty that made me just about lose my lunch. In affiliation with a Christian woman's magazine, a simple post on social media triggered my outrage at the false teachings on modesty I have inherited. When a picture of a short skirt is accompanied with the words, "Slut. Whore. She was asking for it," you can bet we have got it seriously wrong in terms of God's heart for His daughters and their physical appearance.

We need to recognize the difficult truth that much of what we, as Christian women folk, have been taught about modesty is rooted in two things: one, shame and two, guilt.

We are taught to be ashamed of our bodies because we show off too much of them. We learn to replace feeling attractive with feeling guilty because we might cause our brothers in Christ to stumble at the sight of our calves or breasts or butt or whatever it is they stare at. Is there some validity here? Yes, absolutely. There are plenty of temptations for men to stare at in this world—they do not need any more of them when they walk into church on Sunday morning. That is a valid piece of the argument, but that is certainly not the whole picture. We have missed the point of modesty for the sake of results.

Want a woman to change her behavior, like say, how she dresses? The fastest way through that obstacle is guilt—and the enemy is well aware of that. He, too, knows to attack our thoughts if he seeks to influence our behavior. Hence, we have been guilt fed and shamed into layer upon layer of self-preservation; both with what we wear and with our thoughts on our own bodies. That nagging voice you hear when you look maybe just *a little* too good? The false comfort you feel in hiding behind a baggy sweatshirt, because you have substituted your definition of beauty with the number on the scale? The lies in the fitting room that tell you "you'll *never* pull that look off"? Or the one he uses on me the most, "If men don't stare at you in adoration, do you even really matter?"

The enemy has made a mess of modesty, and we have to do the hard and worthy work of cleaning out the junk.

Don't get me wrong, there are some helpful guidelines out there if you are looking to dress modestly. There are even some fantastic, beautiful things to wear these days that don't require underwear the size of dental floss. All helpful, all practical, *but not all rooted in truth.* We have taken something intended to honor the beauty the Lord gave us and twisted it around our hearts like barbed wire—it hurts every time we try to mess with it. The enemy has taken something intended to protect our beauty, and marred it into something that makes us feel as though we must hide it.

The Bible has some things to say about how women dress. To cut your hair, or not to cut your hair? To wear jeans? How about makeup? How about shorts? When is it too much? When is the line crossed? Sorry, ladies. I don't have that answer for you yet. If you come up with one, send it on over, because this modesty thing is a hot (but tastefully covered) mess.

Here is what the Bible actually has to say on the matter:

"Since you are all set apart by God, made holy and dearly loved, clothe yourselves with *a holy way of life*: compassion, kindness, humility, gentleness, and patience." Colossians 3:12

Women, the same goes for you: dress properly, modestly, and appropriately. Do not get carried away in grooming your hair or *seek beauty in* glittering gold, pearls, or expensive clothes. Instead, as is fitting, let good works *decorate your true beauty and* show that you are a woman who claims reverence for God." 1st Timothy 2: 9-10

That is the truth.

Modesty is *not* about being ashamed of your beauty and attempting to hide it as not to distract or derail others. It *is* about understanding that God made you, intentionally, to encapsulate beauty and to be loved just as you are—so you do not need to worry about finding your identity in how you look or what you wear. Though if we were being honest, we would admit that we certainly try, don't we?

True immodesty is idolizing our own appearance. We are immodest when we put our looks above anything else. Isn't that when we are most likely to wear something slightly less "appropriate" anyways? We are immodest when we forget to clothe ourselves in compassion. We are immodest when we forget the Name we carry and the Savior we have living in our hearts.

It all comes down to whose attention we are seeking. Are we trying to manage our image or be an image bearer of the Most High Creator? We are not too far off—it's not even that our answers about modesty are inherently wrong. The problem is that we have been raised to ask the wrong questions. This conversation is flawed from the get-go because it is based on blame and pointing fingers. It should not a debate over whether women should cover up more or men should stare and ogle less—it is about doing your part regardless of your sex to live life in light of being made worthy of the Gospel—and sharing free grace by not passing the buck onto the opposing side of the argument.

You are likely familiar with some of the results of modern-day feminism. If you are, you may have heard some pretty lies about empowerment. You may have been taught that women should feel free to flaunt their bodies, no matter what they look like, because they feel confident and do not succumb to the pressure of societal beauty standards. While half of my heart wants to stand and applaud these efforts—the other half wants to stand up and shout, "*Sit down*. This fight has nothing to do with confidence, you don't know how men see you".

I spent the majority of my time in college surrounded by, well, military men. Some entitled, some sincere, some supportive of me in various leadership roles, and some...not-so-much. However, I did learn quite a bit about how the other half lives during those four years, friend. Let me tell you. It ain't pretty. After a while, I became just like "one of the guys." No longer did a polite bubble of censorship surround me. I heard it all. Saw it all. Experienced the fullest extent of the male college persona. It changed the way I view the battle our brothers are fighting.

I may not have a clinical background in dealing with addiction, and I am no neuroscientist. What I do know is this: men stare. They ogle. They make comments under their breath like you would not believe. If I shared with you even one tenth of what I heard my peers say about the pretty young things who strolled around our campus, you would lose your lunch, spit out your coffee, and proceed to wear turtlenecks for the rest of your life. Trust me on this.

Maybe this knowledge is nothing new to you. To some extent, I surely knew that men stared, and I knew what caught their attention. We all know that, don't we? Anyone else have a third date sweater in their wardrobe that hugs all the right places? What shocked me the most was not the fact that men ogled— that much I knew to expect. It is how *little* it took to set them off that worried me then, and still worries me now. I attended a rather conservative school. Even girls who "didn't cover up much" still probably wore more than the average college gal, if I had to venture a guess. I am not talking about sports bras and spandex at the gym, though that is certainly worthy in the male gaze of commentary. The kind of outfit that elicited the most crude and vile of responses by my male counterparts could be as simple as yoga pants a t-shirt that revealed half an inch of a bra strap. That's it. I am not talking booty shorts and high heels on a Saturday night, or whatever girls wear out these days. I am talking about even the slightest hint of a figure hugging ensemble. That is all it takes. Well intentioned girls who left the house probably thinking that they were dressing modestly enough to avoid such attention, were in fact, on the receiving end of it.

Now, you can hear that nagging tone in my voice when I write about this, yeah? I cannot address the issue of modesty without considering both sides. Again, the goal here is not blame—but mutual understanding of the struggle. These guys I went to college with? They did not wake up one day and start staring at our low-cut tops because they thought to do so on their own. *Their behavior, too, is learned* as part of a societal set of expectations. They, too, feel the pressure of belonging and relating to others based on mutual interest. Unfortunately for us, that mutual interest is often the favorite American past-time of checking out women together in bars or clubs or dance halls or you know, the dorm. But let's not miss this opportunity to call it what it is—what our society deems appropriate, acceptable, and even affirming for women, the Bible identifies as lust. Longing for something that ain't yours. Remember King David and Bathsheba, anyone? This is not a new struggle—it has been around since the Psalms. Literally. This is an age-old battle fought against men. Us women folk are most assuredly the casualties. As are the marriages and relationships and families that this lust has torn apart. It is not innocent. It is not cute. It is not flattering. It is sin, and it is worth our time spent discussing it as such.

Hopefully you can see that we are all caught up in the same battle, and we have to get it into our heads that it is *not* against each other. We are being shot down on all sides. Case and point? When the swimsuit edition of Sport's Illustrated hits the shelves, nobody wins. Men lose when they are given yet another falsely perfect temptation to stare at, and we women lose because we are given another false expectation to live up to.

Are you seeing this picture yet? Men are not the enemy. Our bikinis are not the enemy. It all comes back to our thought life; what men think of us when we dress certain ways and what we think of ourselves when we do not feel good enough to.

There came a moment in time when the Lord convicted me on my, um, *questionable* wardrobe choices. I had a closet full of tight little dresses and low-cut tops and you know what? I felt really good in them. However, and this is important, the reasons I felt so good in them are the *same* reasons I should not have been wearing them in the first place. When I hit the bars in those outfits, a sentence I can hardly believe I'm actually writing, I knew *exactly* what kind of attention I would draw. I knew what I was doing, and therein lies the real problem.

This brings us back to the issue of the heart, if you will come full circle with me here. The problem is almost never the dress. It is the reasons we choose to put it on. We know that men will stare, buy us drinks, and try to win our approval. I acted this way to pad a deflated ego after a bad breakup and my goodness, haven't we all done that? A harmless girls' night where you just want to feel good about yourself? It seems so incredibly harmless. I know because I have done it countless times, but what I want us to grasp is that this act is not innocent on either side. Just as our brothers should not lust after our bodies, we should not put it all out there for them to freely lust after.

The battle for their minds is hard enough.
The battle against our self-esteem is hard enough.
Stop fighting.
Stop advancing the issue.
Stop playing into the enemy's hands because you think looking like that will somehow increase your value.

We both know that it won't. Not for a single moment.

Reality check? Every time I put on an outfit like that, I was telling God that He was not enough to define me. I was proclaiming, rather loudly, that I needed validation from something other than the work done for me on the cross to feel good about myself. I was implying—no, saying clearly, that redemption was not enough to satisfy my selfish desire for immediate approval from the men of this world. It is not about the dress. It almost never is. Modesty is a heart issue; not a wardrobe issue, and it is time we start treating it that way.

In terms of dressing appropriately, I used to think there was some magical, secret middle ground reserved for those "really Godly women." Surely there was some mystical, enchanted place where I was aware of my flaws, felt beautiful anyways, and never flaunted it in a way that would cause anyone to "stumble" down a flight of lust-filled concrete stairs. Does anyone know where that place is? Because I haven't found it yet.

What I have found, however, is much more captivating—much more freeing. I have found that when my focus is on Jesus and what He has redeemed in me, I feel beautiful. All the way at the core of my being—I feel delighted in. Cherished. Fought for. Claimed as His daughter. This is the kind of beauty that even a bad case of PMS and sweatpants cannot touch. This is the place where appreciation of how the Lord made me can freely flow. And it has nothing to do with shame, condemnation, guilt, or a dang Victoria's Secret catalog.

This is where much of my frustration lies. Growing up in the Church—no one ever told me modesty was about honoring the beauty the Lord gave me. No one ever told me it was about so much more than hiding behind layers of baggy clothes and desperately wanting someone to notice you.

It is about honoring the beauty Maker.

Stop and think for a second. Go back to some of the most incredible scenes you've taken in. Was it a mountain? A sunset? The smile on a child's face overseas? Whatever it is—I'll bet you anything, you were stunned by the beauty of that moment. I'll bet it stopped you in your tracks. I'll bet you get chills just thinking about it. *That is exactly what beauty does:* It elicits a response. Our response to those moments is almost unmistakably the purest form of worship to our Creator God. We stand in awe of the beautiful moments He creates for us.

Let me tell you—just as those mountains and beaches and sunsets are reflections of the beauty of the Glory of God—so are you. You reflect and encapsulate that same beauty. Will you take a moment, here? Can we pause, put our books and coffee down, and reflect? I want you to really grasp this before we move on.

The beauty in you is innate—*it is a part of you that cannot be removed.* It is a part of the fabric of your being, as you are made in His image. It cannot be taken away---and the enemy knows that. Since Satan does not posses the ability to actually strip it from us, he seeks to alter our perception of it. To twist our expectations for it. To poison our thoughts about it. I'd say he's done a decent job—but don't lose heart; the final war has already been won for us. Our beauty lives on to fight another day.

A big part of unlearning our thoughts on modesty is recognizing that the beauty the Lord created you with is constantly under attack. We have taken good and scriptural concepts and spilled them over into the enemy's game plan to derail our confidence. It is a huge mess—and it will take a lot of work to separate the two. Now we are trapped between feeling inadequate when we wake up in sweatpants with messy hair, but also too prideful on the days we actually wear makeup and wear a killer outfit.

How do I feel humble enough to reflect Jesus, but confident enough to not feel pathetic?
When is it too much?
When do I cross the line from confident to prideful?
When am I allowed to feel beautiful?

These questions from my heart, and probably yours, too are evidence of the war that has been waged on beauty.

Oh, yes. When the enemy plays tricks, he plays dirty. We know from the truth of the Bible that he seeks to steal, kill and destroy. That is, he seeks to kill our confidence by saturating our culture with false standards of beauty. He tries to steal our beauty by marring it under layers of comparison games and magazine ads and workout routines and Pinterest feeds. He tries to destroy our understanding of beauty by replacing it with worldly things—a flatter stomach, toned legs, whiter teeth, longer hair, and clearer skin. It is a nasty, nasty battle. So what are we going to do about it? We are going to unlearn, and it has to start now.

Take that ideal version of yourself that you are constantly striving towards. Now, dethrone it. I am completely serious. Burn the magazine, throw away the scale, delete the dang Pinterest workout board you made but never use, and throw away those dumb high school jeans you haven't worn since you were 14, and take off your makeup while you're at it. Those things do not define you, so get rid of them.

And now it is time to replace them with the truth.

Every Word in scripture has its place. Some, apply more so to an older context, but that doesn't mean we can't dig out the good stuff. After all, God's Word remains eternal. His wisdom does not change with the seasons. So even if you are familiar with this passage in reference to modesty, please do not roll your eyes and gloss past this. There is something for us, here.

**"Do not focus on decorating your exterior by doing your hair or putting on fancy jewelry or wearing fashionable clothes; let your adornment be what's inside—*the real you,* the lasting beauty of a gracious and quiet spirit, in which God delights."
1st Peter 3:3-4**

What interests me most in the above passages is this:
We are not *really* that different from the women of biblical
times in regards to how we view beauty. They were told,
specifically, not to find their beauty in the braiding of their hair
or in the wearing of jewelry—not to avoid such things all
together. There were vain women then, there are vain women
now. We still exist, ya dig? The women Paul was writing to in
these verses were incredibly concerned with their appearance.
That's what they did, that's who they were. His urging here is
not necessarily to put off practices of doing your hair or makeup
or whatever it is that you do—his urging is not to find your
beauty in it. We are encouraged to not limit our beauty to our
morning routine, because it is so much *more* than that.

Maybe these verses are not as far removed from applying to us
as we thought, yeah? Bottom line is this, your hair is your hair.
Your face is your face. Do with them what you want. Just don't
fall into the trap of depending on a good hair day or your
favorite concealer to feel good about yourself.

While I have you here, talking about societal constructs of
beauty, let me say this: The number on the scale does not now,
and never will, define you. We have *so many* younger girls
looking to us to figure out what beautiful is. Let us be mindful of
where we are leading them. Your body is a temple, so treat it
well. Treat yourself with kindness and the upmost care. Make
that temple last, cause it's the only one you get. Rather than
challenging yourself to lose an absurd amount of weight or wear
a size zero or to look like someone else—try framing your goals
in terms of gaining strength, in caring for your body.

Forget the size two jeans you have needlessly been told you
need to fit into. Forget the commercials and magazine ads that
represent fewer than one percent of the population. Remember
to show yourself some grace, and to take good care of you.
Everything in moderation? That includes dieting, exercising, and
the lengths we go to when we attempt to look like someone

else's version of pretty.
Actually. Don't do that last one at all. Got it?

I am sure that most of us have heard the phrase, "real beauty is on the inside," before. But what does that even *mean*? It is vague, I do not fully grasp it, and our culture does not reflect that as true. Our Christian role models do not reflect that as true. Really, have you *seen* the ways we get dolled up for our women's conferences? We all think beauty is on the outside; we are unsure of how to look for it on the inside, so we are convinced we must just not have enough of it, right?

This is why I would like the frame this "beauty" concept in a new way. I do not want us to fall into the pattern of thought that says *because* beauty is internal it therefore *must be hidden*. This hints, ever so slightly, that beauty is to be reserved and not outwardly expressed, that people must look, and look hard, to see your beauty. By no means is this the case. We have misinterpreted this idea of beauty it its entirety. We took a word used to describe God Himself and made a mess of it. Now, it is covered in lipstick stains and mascara goop.

Let me ask you this, why is God beautiful? Have you seen His face? Do you know how much He weighs? What about His hair color, His jean size, or His complexion? If beauty is used to describe a God without revealing specific, physical attributes, how do we think we can define our beauty by examining our own?

Beauty is not about physical appearance. Beauty is not even limited to your personality, it is your very character. Beauty is *what you do*. Beauty is *who you are*. Beauty is an attribute of God Himself—and you reflect that. You harness that in your heart as a daughter who bears His name. Our culture says beauty *looks*; the Bible says beauty *does*. It is action and attribute, yes, but not solely appearance. We must reclaim this word and restore to it the original intent—to describe who we are, not what our mirror shouts at us each morning.

Take all of the lies about modesty and beauty you've got in that intellectual and capable head of yours. Dump them out, here. I want you to dig deep and think hard—what has this world told you about being "beautiful"? Do these things make you feel more like the honored, uniquely crafted woman that you are? If they don't—leave 'em on the pages of this book and do not dare to pick them up again.

It will take time to purge this mess from our hearts, I get that. So while we are dumping all this junk about, let us lift our eyes to the Most High Savior. We can pray that He will refine and renew our sense of beauty. Ask that He will empty us of these worldly standards and give us something much more worthy of holding on to—a desire to see His beauty in all of its forms. In the mirror, in the streets, in the women around us as they do life. Pray that our time would not be spent idolizing a new figure or hairstyle or wardrobe, but rather, looking up to know more of who God is and more of His heart behind making us the beautiful, strong women that we are.

P.S. You never need anyone's permission, acceptance, or praise to feel beautiful *(not even your own)*.

Questions for Unlearning

- What has your definition of beauty looked like until now?

- What has been your ideal—the "perfect version" of yourself that you've been working for?

- Where do you look for validation for your physical appearance? How do you feel when you find that validation? How about when you don't?

- Has any part of your physical appearance become an idol, something you can't feel complete without perfecting or managing each day?

- What are some practical steps you can take to dethrone these idols?

Challenge Five

I can already tell you...you *probably* don't want to do this. You're going to laugh it off, roll your eyes, and tell me that it is a *super lame* challenge and I must have run out of ideas to put *this* at the end of the chapter. Humor me, anyways, alright? This part is here for a reason, I guarantee you.

I need you to write out all the things you love about yourself-- physical appearance, personality, talents, all of it. Yes. I am completely serious, and yes, I know that we are not in junior high. Though since we are being honest, we can admit that the last time we did this probably *was* junior high. It's time we update that list, hmm?

So stop avoiding it, get your pen, and get ready to write.

I have left plenty of room for you on the next page, because my hope is that once you start writing out your beauty—it will flow out of you as praise unto the Lord. You can thank Him for the ways he has made you beautiful. You can thank Him for revealing beauty to you in new ways. You can cry at all the beauty you have missed in desperate attempts to look like someone else; someone "better". You can do whatever you would like in this challenge, because this journey *is* yours, deal?

Regardless of what you choose to write, you and I both know, when it comes to the way we view beauty: *something's gotta give.* That is what this space is for—to start unlearning.

So get to it, beautiful.

Things I Love About Myself

Let Us Pray

Father, we come before you repentant of all the things we've tried to find validation in that didn't depend on you. We are here because we know, deep down, that beauty is so much more than the images we are constantly bombarded with. We know that you have intended to show your glory and beauty through our lives and today, we are turning away from the habits that derail us from that focus. Lord we thank you for the beauty you demonstrate in your creation. We thank you for the reminders that beauty is all around us, in us, and done through us by our actions. We thank you and praise you for being a God who delights in sunsets and mountains and scenes that give us glimpses of shalom; of wholeness and peace.

We thank you for using us in all of our mess to demonstrate your beauty to the world around us. We ask that you change our thinking. Change our perceptions of beauty so that we no longer live a life enslaved by Pinterest feeds and weight loss and our makeup bags. We ask that you give us a shift in thinking, and in the ways we talk about beauty with the women around us. Let us be women that encourage bold actions before we encourage highlights and a new haircut. Let us ask questions of each other about spiritual health before anything else. Let us acknowledge the beauty in other women around us, and not fall victim to the never-ending comparison games we are surrounded with in our culture. Let other people see this change in us. Let it point them to you, to your love, and to your ability to supernaturally change our hearts.

We ask this, in full confidence and faith, because you are a loving Father that withholds no good thing from your children. We are completely dependent on you for any change to take place in our hearts and minds, and we ask that you grow our ability to see beauty—instead of limiting a word used to describe your creation to the things we see on the cover of a magazine. We pray for protection over our minds as we step into this season of searching for beauty. We declare that the lies we are so caught up in will have no authority over us. We boldly proclaim that your victory has been won over our thoughts, and that the enemy's tricks and cheap shots will not steal our momentum or our focus. We ask that you guide us, Lord. As we seek this new understanding, give us wisdom. Give us truth to hold onto. Remind us that because of who you are, we are free. We are free to be beautiful in all of its forms.

A Good Wife

We cannot very well have a book on Christian femininity if we leave out the elephant in the room.

We need to talk marriage; but not in the ways we have been taught to talk about it. We need to be open about the struggle it can be to join your life with someone else's. We need to talk about the hard parts and the dark places and the moments of weakness, and the days we put the desire to win the argument above the promise to love our spouse.

When I was twenty, I thought I had found "the one" and that marriage was going to be a walk in the park. I seriously wish someone would have slapped me upside the head. Take note: this park is full of closed roads and broken streetlamps, and some days it is more of an uphill climb than a casual stroll. I am thankful I realized he was *not* the one for me *before* we made an irrevocable commitment to walk this life out together.

Let's face it--marriage is hard.

We can say that out loud and maybe we should do so more often. This is no way discounts its beauty or intricacy, though. What good and lovely thing has ever come easily? We should be confident in saying that our marriage has challenged us—forced us to grow up in ways we did not anticipate. Forced us to love our closest friend through times of unthinkable brokenness. Forced us to be a voice of reason in the midst of chaos. Forced us to learn how to love in incredible and unexpected ways.

"Consider the lilies of the field, how they grow," Jesus says in

Matthew 6: 28-29, **"They do not work or weave or sew, *and yet their garments are stunning.* Even King Solomon, dressed in his most regal garb, was not as lovely as these lilies."**

When marriage is lined up with the Word, God can and does make it beautiful. However, *we* are still the ones who need to do the growing and the stretching.

By God's grace, and after a lot of unlearning, I married my best friend on a Tuesday morning wearing my favorite dress. I have been happily joined at the heart with Taylor for nearly two years. Prior to that, we spent a year cultivating our friendship and letting the Lord guide our dating relationship. Six months out of that we spent, quite literally, on opposite sides of the globe while I served overseas. Our relationship during that time was based on a lot of praying, and few and far between skype dates over patchy South African internet. When I got home, marriage was the next step the Lord had for us, and I am grateful beyond words for this man who takes the covenant agreement we made with God as seriously as I do.

So, when I speak to my generation especially, I am drawing from my own somewhat immediate experience. However, I am also drawing heavily on the real life experience of others who influenced my growing-up years with ideals and actualities of marriage that had a direct impact on my perception and understanding. Y'all. I have seen some *tough* situations. I have been caught in the middle of some un-good and un-lovely marriage struggles that affected me directly because they affected people I love. This sort of history is so common to my generation, and to many of my friends who are now in the developing stages of their own marriages and life stories. I have consulted with older women who have been at this wife thing for a while now. I have sought honest input from my peers who are no longer quite newlyweds. When I say we, I mean all of us—and we all need to unlearn some things about marriage, specifically Christian marriage. Having said that, we will continue with this:

It is okay if you think marriage is hard.
It is *both* a worthy challenge *and* a holy climb.
It was never intended to be convenient.
The difference in where we are now and where we are headed?
All of the mileage you put into your marriage should actually
lead somewhere.

Fret not, you are not about to be compared to the Proverbs 31
woman. I am not here to tell you all the ways you are failing as a
wife. I am not going to list out your perceived womanly duties
and hold them over your head like a banner of failure to guilt
you into submission—because that won't do you any good.

If you think in any way like I do, you are already well aware of
the ways that you fail. You list them out all the time, constantly
trying to "measure up," to some impossible standard of
perfection, right? Let us put down our filters for a moment. Let
us stop criticizing ourselves and seek to view this larger picture,
this intricate tapestry.

It is time to *really* talk about marriage.

As we dig into this topic, there is a clear distinction that needs
to be made. You see, the confusion and hurt run so deep, we
must address unlearning our thoughts on marriage from many
angles. We need to unlearn both the lies we have come to
believe *about* marriage, yes, but also our own junk we have
created *within* it.

The first key in the unlearning is to challenge the societal and
religious falsities that we have learned to embrace about
marriage as an institution. Our view of this bigger picture is a
little hazy. We are all looking at marriage, yes, but we are doing
so through a dirty window that's full of smudges and keeps us
from seeing God's design for it clearly. This is why hearing
words like "submission" and "sacrifice" make us cringe like nails
on a chalkboard. This is why we get the gnawing feeling in our

stomachs that if we did not marry, we would not matter.

The easy sell of marriage is widely bought without question in our culture. If you love someone, they make you happy, and you are willing to bet half of your stuff that they will stick with you forever, chances are you should *probably* get married. We rely on "signs" that he really is "the one" using trivial factors like his favorite flavor of ice cream of the fact that you met at "just the right time," instead of looking at his spiritual maturity and potential ability to be a godly support when life gets hard. We use our feelings, our fleeting and flesh-driven feelings, to make important permanent decisions about the guy we want to marry. Why? Because we cannot stop picturing the *perfect* minimalist ring that we found six months ago on Etsy, and we have become so infatuated with ideas about our chic-yet-rustic wedding day that we fail to plan the marriage that comes with it.

I say this because it seems our generation in particular has come to emphasize the wedding itself with great significance, while leaving little preparation or thought regarding the covenant and responsibility marriage entails. Maybe if we were honest, some of us would admit that all we really wanted was a pretty dress, some professional photos to show off on social media, and an excuse to validate an excessive number of hours browsing Pinterest. The mandate of submission and the hard work of unpacking our spouse's baggage was never on the schedule, it wasn't even in the destination brochure. We just want a big party where we are dressed to the nines and get lots of presents. It may seem harsh, but having lived this reality myself, I can tell you that this mentality exists. It makes the biblical understanding of marriage seem far less appealing from the outside looking in, because it looks more like serving and sacrificing, and less like the end of a Katherine Heigel movie.

Even in our churches, we see some flawed thinking when it comes to this holy covenant. I believe we have been taught to idolize marriage, both from pulpits and from our Christian community at large. That's right, *marriage* can be an idol, and a really attractive one at that. We see this in the ways members of singles group appear to be pitied; as if unmarried men and women appear to hold less validity in ministry. Somehow, once we get married, our opinions begin to hold more weight. We see this in the ways the still singles in singles' ministries are almost overtly talked down to by those of us with rings on our left hands, as the group of thirty-somethings shares donuts on a Sunday morning trying to figure out why God has not yet "blessed them" with a spouse. We see this in the ways such great emphasis is placed on young women to learn to be godly wives in their twenties instead of learning to live boldly for the Gospel. Granted, marriage often indicates an increased level of stability in young adults. And, young women not instructed by the time they reach their twenties may be in for quite a shock if they choose to become married without due preparation. But the question remains: Who has time for other forms of ministry when you are consumed with learning how to be a homemaker for your future husband? When we place the ideal of marriage before the importance of being equipped to share the Gospel and finding fulfillment in Christ, we have made it an idol.

This is why, if we are not careful, we can mistakenly wait until marriage to allow ourselves to receive happiness, feel complete, and find our identity. So when we get back down the aisle and marriage does not have the answers we have so desperately been waiting for, we get angry because marriage did not turn out to be the easy fix for our problems we thought it would be. As effortless as it can be to do, it is not okay to depend on our spouses for happiness. This is unbiblical, and another form of idolization in a very real sense, as it places your spouse in much too high a place that only needs to be inhabited by our true Savior. This is also unwise, unhealthy, and impractical, as he is human and prone to failure.

Since the making of marriage into an idol is so wrong, why do we continue down the same beaten path? Well, this is what we are taught, yes, but it is also what our sinful nature desires. Our spouse has the potential to provide the attention, approval, and physical comfort that our flesh so strongly craves. In and of itself, this is not a bad thing. After all, God said it is not good for man to be alone. Our husbands *should* love and cherish us, absolutely. But we cannot expect them to ascribe to us our worth nor endow us with value. That is not their job. That is God's gift to us when we pursue His will for our lives. What our spouse should provide is the spiritual support required by scripture to keep us moving closer to Christ. When we seek to base our happiness on another person, particularly a spouse who has such a direct influence on us, we will always come up empty-handed and disappointed.

The damage can start earlier than we think, friend. Long before the infamous first fight and months before we learn the art of slamming doors, we have been set up for failure if we have not been taught to consciously fight the making of marriage into an idol.

After the first dance, a few flutes of champagne, and the glorious week in West Palm, we get home from our honeymoons to a rude awakening. Our spouse has not magically changed upon saying their vows, and neither have we. We made it down the aisle, yes, but our groom now seems glaringly imperfect and somewhere in the depths of our core, this makes us angry. The one person who was supposed to make us happy and whole and finally complete our life looks far less appealing when he sports the same cargo shorts for three days than he did in that wedding day tux. Are we really supposed to submit to this guy that still wears superhero themed socks and does not own a can opener? *Excuse me, Lord, there must be a mistake.*

So the dishes and resentment start to pile up, and we fall into our newlywed routines. We equate our understanding of spousal submission with the cleanliness of our kitchen floors and do not investigate any further. We forget the vows we made to love humbly and sacrificially as we bitterly make pasta for the fifth night in a row while our husbands blindly assume that all is well. We stop communicating, and therefore stop growing. At this point, we have already done the most damage we can do to our marriages, because we have carried the expectations of society's ideals into them instead of genuine joyful obedience to the Lord's design.

For those of you several years deep into your covenant, you may start to see the ways these expectations and misunderstandings have acted as a poison in your own relationship with your spouse. This is why we also must allow space to unlearn the habits and lies we have come to embrace *within* our marriages. If you are tired of having the same old frivolous arguments, like what to watch on Netflix or where to eat for dinner; or if you feel trapped in the cycles of mutually allowing sin however big or small because you've learned it is just not worth the time and energy it takes to combat it, this is for you. Be warned, complacency can become a sinful stronghold that can spiral quickly out of control. Some of you need to address issues with your spouse that are far more severe than fighting over pizza toppings or which way the toilet paper should roll. Realities such as addiction, abuse, and infidelity *absolutely* need to be challenged, but challenged *safely*. I urge you to seek counsel from your pastoral staff or from a professional counselor. Know that it is not wrong, weak, or a sin to ask for help, and that you are perfectly within the boundaries of scripture to seek assistance, set boundaries, and protect yourself.

Though we may have missed God's intent for marriage early on, the beauty of grace is that we can always change our course. We can choose to identify the lies we believe, and ask the Lord to remove them. We can work alongside our spouses to repair the damage done by them. We can fight for our marriages and watch as God does the unthinkable. We can and will see our marriages restored.

The root of the issue here is that when our idolized marriage fails to make us happy, as our upbringing falsely taught us that it would, we fall into a hopeless and self-blaming mindset that *we must be doing something wrong*. If we were "good enough" as wives, our husbands would make us feel complete. If we were with the *right person*, this marriage stuff would be easy, and our marriage alone would be enough to satisfy. Surely, if we were doing all that we are supposed to do as women, our marriage would somehow be better. It would not be so...hard. So lonely. So much *less* than we pictured in our young minds when we bought the white dress that collects dust in our guest room closet.

And so we start the brutal and debilitating habit of viewing ourselves as a burden to our husband, like an emotional leach that drains him with our incessant nagging and need for validation. This is the damage of idolizing marriage; of looking to our spouse to fill a void that is far too wide and far too deep for any one man to conquer. We have invited sin and idolatry into our marriage beds, and they will grow like weeds if they remained unchallenged.

The happy ending that we expected to blossom overnight is nowhere to be found, as this marriage business turns out to be much harder work than we are taught to expect. This is how the world's definition of marriage, and the church's silence in opposing it, leads to brutal divorces because we wake up at 50 and nothing has changed.

So how can we stop the snowball from turning into a full-blown avalanche that buries our marriage in its wake?

We need to first reset our minds with the understanding that our spouse is not the enemy. We are one team, fighting for the same advancement in our marriage. Make no mistake, there is indeed a battlefield, but we should always be standing on the same side of it. Until we can fully accept that, we will have trouble moving forward.

God's design for marriage is one that should inspire growth in us, even intimidate us, once we fully understand its implications. We must now seek a renewed understanding of one, God's purpose for marriage, and two, our roles within this covenant.

When we look at the famously referenced passage in Ephesians about marriage, we get a picture that vastly contrasts the modern rhetoric about wedded life. As we have discussed, the prevailing cultural norm regarding marriage is that it must be self-pleasing; its purpose is to make us happy. What we see in the Word flips this script on marriage, and dares us to view our covenant in light of eternity, in light of sanctification and pursuing Christ. It might sound slightly less romantic than long walks on the beach and candlelit dinners, but when we press into the truth, we will see a challenging and beautiful definition of marriage come to life.

And the Spirit makes it possible to submit *humbly* to one another out of respect for the Anointed. Wives, *it should be no different* with your husbands. Submit to them as you do to the Lord, for God has given husbands a *sacred* duty to lead as the Anointed leads the church and serves as the head. (The church is His body; He is her Savior.) So wives should submit to their husbands, *respectfully,* in all things, just as the church yields to the Anointed One. Husbands, you must love your wives so *deeply, purely, and sacrificially that we can understand it only when we* compare it to the love the Anointed One has for *His bride,* the church. *We know* He gave Himself up completely to make her His own, washing her clean of all her impurity with water and *the powerful presence of* His word. *He has given Himself* so that He can present the church as His radiant bride, unstained, unwrinkled, and unblemished—*completely free from all impurity*—holy and innocent before Him. So husbands should care for their wives *as if their lives depended on it,* the same way they care for their own bodies. As you love her, you ultimately are loving *part of* yourself *(remember, you are one flesh).* No one really hates his own body; he takes care to feed and love it, just as the Anointed takes care of His church, because we are *living* members of His body. 'And this is the reason a man leaves his father and his mother and is united with his wife; the two come together as one flesh.' There is a great mystery *reflected* in this *Scripture,* and I say that it has to do with *the marriage of* the Anointed One and the church. Nevertheless, each husband is to love *and protect* his own wife as if she were his very heart, and each wife is to respect her own husband. Ephesians 5:21-33

Where the world tells us marriage is about seeking happiness through spousal gratification, the Word claims marriage is about seeking holiness, achieved through sanctification. Can you see the stark contrast yet? Marriage should propel us forward towards Christ, and provide an increased understanding of the love He has for His bride, the church.

Understanding this truth is crucial to an eternal view of matrimony:
Your marriage is not now, and will never be, about you.

Harsh? Yes.
True? Absolutely.

Your marriage *is* about mirroring the love Christ has for His bride, and seeking to draw others into His family by being an example of that very same love. The construct of marriage and family serves as a microcosm of the body of Christ, beautiful and designed for glory, not for self-gratification. Your marriage can actually *refute* the chaos we see in unions not joined together in the pursuit of the Lord. In other words—there *should be* a marked difference in the way believers treat their spouses. People should know Who we represent based on the *ways we love our husbands.*

Wait, what?

If that thought intimidates the heck out of you, you are not alone. If someone were to look objectively at the way I love Taylor, and judge my salvation based on that alone, you bet I would be in big trouble. This change in mentality is a big leap, and it will take time to reframe our thoughts as we move forward.

I know it seems like a difficult task. We have some big shoes to fill, indeed, when it comes to having a marriage in step with the Spirit. The scriptural truth may be a tall order, but my prayer is that we will not miss the miracle of marriage because it looks more like hard work than happily ever after. Maybe the hard work *is* the happily ever after, not because it is hard on us, but because it brings the best *out of* us. That's the amazing thing about marriage in light of eternity--when it all lines up according to God's design, you *do* get the blessing. You get to enjoy the benefits of marriage and the joy that comes with doing life alongside your best friend.

This why I can promise you that it is well worth the effort to unlearn the junk we have in our hearts about marriage and submission and our roles as wives who seek Christ above all else. The return on investment, in both a temporal and eternal perspective, is more than we can fathom. It is going to be hard work, yes, but this is absolutely worth our time. Our husbands and our marriages are worth our time, because in the end, our Lord is glorified and He is definitely worth our time.

When we begin to view marriage from an eternal standpoint, we will eternally be reaping the benefits. If our focus is on living out the Gospel in the context of our marriages so that others might come to know Christ by the way we love and treat each other, it leaves little room to be mad when the toilet seat is left up. It makes those arguments we have about how to best load the dishwasher look like a joke, because we are focused on the bigger mission entrusted to us.

One of the biggest things hindering that mission is this marred and muddy idea of our roles in marriage. Because we do not fully understand God's intent for the words "submission" and "sacrifice," we hide behind layers of societal clichés about gender and assume that they are scriptural. We, as women, are angry that we have to submit because we have been taught that it means to be weak, to be lesser, and to be second. We do not like the sound of those words, am I right?

We are often told that it is biblical to submit without question, but the truth is that most of us do not want to submit at all. We view it simultaneously as both a dirty word and a scriptural mandate. Not only is this rock heavy, but we have no desire to lug it around. I don't know about you, but my knee-jerk and prideful feminist reaction is "Hell, no, I will not submit. I am an equal to my husband and I deserve to be treated as such. Why can't he iron his own dang shirts?" This is because I, too, have certainly messed with the truth of the Word to make it fit into society's mold of being a "good wife."

The first problem I see for us with submission, as we know it, is that is has become synonymous with societal constructs of gender. If it is socially and historically suggested that the women's job to do the housework and rear the children in the home, then the church took this into overdrive.

The intentions? Absolutely pure.
The result? Anything but.

The church took some wonderful, incredibly beautiful passages about our role of being a wife and you know what? It got all mixed in with cultural demands and pressures for women and mothers. It is as if a three-year-old got their hands on their two favorite colors of play-dough, and now we cannot separate the two without ruining the whole wad of it. I'd say the resulting color is pretty dang ugly, right?

The main reason we cringe at this thought of submission is that we have learned, be it through society or personal experience, that it does not always pan out the way we hoped it would. Whether you saw your mother struggle to raise children on her own, you had a passive or absent father, an abusive father, or have been hurt by other men in your life—the pain caused by these men echoes our prideful flesh to say, "Do not trust. Do not submit. You are only ever going to get hurt in this arrangement. This does not end well for you."

While the truth behind submission whispers the hope that marriage is a safe place, where you can trust, our experience and cynicism shout back that it simply cannot be so.

If we took the courage to speak absolute truth on the matter, we would admit that most of us are not only peeved by the idea of submission, but we are also afraid of it. Granted, that fear has validity to you. It is based on your previous, often negative experiences with men. So you have, knowingly or unknowingly, created a way to prevent the pain and manage the fear.

We have labeled this fear as "independence" and walked away with our heads held high, but hear this from someone who has been down this road: there is nothing strong or trendy or empowering about being married to someone that you cannot lean on when the going gets tough, and we have established that it undoubtedly will pour like hell at one time or another.

So, what does it really mean to submit to your husband?

In reality, this idea of submitting has a lot *less* to do with washing dishes and ironing shirts and a lot *more* to do with respecting the godly man you have decided to marry. Titus chapter 2 does *not* say that women must *always* stay home with the children, can *only* wash the dishes, cook the meals and clean the bathrooms, and can *never* work outside the home. Those ideas come from gender scripts within a traditional mentality and have nothing to do with God-honoring submission. The Word *actually* says that women are to *manage* their households, *respect* their husbands, and *love* their children. What we equate with socially-scripted actions regarding women's roles, the Word equates with an attitude of respect and humility.

Did you hear that? Submission is an attitude of respect and humility, not a never-ending to-do list meant to burden you, or to keep you busy with duty while your husband lives his own life. I pray you can feel some of the weight leave your shoulders as you start to embrace the truth.

If submission is indeed about trusting that the man you married is under God's leadership and direction, then humility becomes essential to the equation. We cannot submit ourselves to someone-we do not respect, and this is where the Word asks us to do the hard part. All of those great lines about love in 1st Corinthians that you read at your wedding? We have to actually live those out with our spouse. We cannot submit ourselves to someone while actively keeping a tally of their wrongdoings, nor can we submit to someone we are needlessly holding grudges against. It is up to us to do the hard and necessary work of giving our spouse a clean slate to work from if we really want to untangle our marriages from the lies we have bought into.

Given that we truly want to respect our husbands, and trust that God has enabled them to take the spiritual lead in our homes, we cannot view them as the villain. The real villain is the enemy of our souls, and he enjoys the disintegration of marriage because it disintegrates the body of Christ. Our husband's role, as defined by the Word, is to love us so sacrificially, it is as if they are embodying the love Christ has for His church. If someone loves you like *that,* do you really need to fear submitting to them?

The second key to unlearning this fear is to remember that we have been made one flesh. We so often forget this truth in a world that screams we must maintain our independence. I am all for having things you do on your own without your spouse. I value my space in my marriage, and we both have accepted that sometimes it is good to spend time apart or to have separate interests. I am no licensed marriage counselor, but I do not see any red flags in this line of thinking. Our mistake is taking this separation of schedules and activities to mean that what happens to us does not affect our spouse. We act as though we are still leading lives that are fully independent of one another. This line of thinking leads us to believe that our sin does not affect our spouse, and to assume that our bad attitudes and spiritual stagnation do not impact them, either.

This is not a truth to be glossed over or taken lightly. While attacking our seemingly-separate spouse in our moments of weakness may feel like the easy way out, we are really hurting ourselves and our marriages in the process. This is what happens when we view our husband as the villain instead of remembering that we have been joined with him at the heart. This is why we need to change our thinking. We have to remember that marriage is not a fight to the death; it is 'till death do us part.

So now that we have cleared up our misconceptions about marriage, it is time to take a good, hard look at the specific lies that are derailing our progress. Then we can get started down the path of unlearning them.

Some of these lies may come from flawed habits of thinking about marriage that were drilled into your head from the way you were raised. This is where our parents have some real potential to screw us up, and by the way, it is okay if you feel like they did. Heck, *their* parents probably didn't have it all figured out, either. Thankfully there is enough grace to go around and enough time to unpack the baggage.

So when it comes to your marriage, specifically, there are likely some beliefs that have been in place long before the day you put the top tier of the cake into the freezer. These lies that we have repeatedly told ourselves have undermined God's beautiful intent for marriage. They have taught us to think and feel negatively towards our spouses, ourselves, and our marriages in general because they are not rooted in truth and they do not lead us back to the cross.

They can sound like many things for you, but these are some examples that come to my mind when I reflect on my own story. Maybe they will resonate with you, too.

This is the hard and good part where we can begin to unlearn the deeper issues, and pull the weeds up by their roots.

If you were raised in a very legalistic religious environment, you may still believe that you are unworthy of love, and therefore, a godly marriage. Sadly, it is also very likely you believe that you are stuck with whatever kind of marriage you got, and if it is not good it is probably your fault, anyway, because you are really only worthy of hell and do not deserve to be any kind of happy on this earth.

Whatever forgiveness you have not accepted, whatever guilt you are needlessly carrying, and whatever sin has snuck its way into your heart and your marriage, you need to hear that you can be free from it. We have not been set free to return to our chains, friend. Whatever lie from the enemy that has you convinced you are unworthy or unlovable, is just that, a lie. The truth of God's Word says that you are undoubtedly worthy because He has made you worthy. You are loved because He has shown you love, even dying for you while you lived in sin. He has purposed your life and joined your heart with your spouse; and He did not do so by mistake.

The danger in believing this lie, that we are unworthy of the marriage we have been brought into, is that it makes us grasp at straws to find our identity. We begin our journey into marriage feeling as if we are lacking, that we are burdens, and that it is up to our spouse to complete us. It is as if we feel we must pay off the debt of being unworthy. This damaging mentality leads us to strive towards the unattainable goal of being a "perfect wife" so that we might somehow become worthy of our husbands.

This shifts our focus inward, causing us to dwell on our own shortcomings. Thus our thoughts about marriage stray far from the truth and seek to feed our flesh and all of its selfish desires. This turns our hearts from an attitude of humility, seeking to love our husbands well, and turns it into an unquenchable thirst for their approval and our own happiness. It takes all of our focus on "we" and transforms it into the lens of, "but what about me?"

The "me first" mentality invites strife, dissent, and division, as we are unable to see things from our husband's point of view. When we put ourselves first in the marriage covenant, chaos quickly follows. A selfish and approval-seeking heart leaves little room for compassion, sacrificial love, or being attentive to the needs of our husbands. So while we work tirelessly towards perfection, hoping to earn whatever it is that we feel we are lacking, we confuse our husbands and leave them in the dark to wonder why nothing they do is good enough to make us happy.

When all of our striving gets us nowhere, we take our spouses silence to mean that they do not care. We believe they would run away from our mess, from our dark corners, if they really knew about our internal struggle for validation. So we are both left empty-handed as we pursue this misunderstanding of a marriage.

This is when we will no longer challenge each other away from sin. We will no longer have open, honest communication about our hearts and how we are feeling. Our conversations turn from talks of scripture and building up one another into quarrels about meaningless things because we have run out of things to say that do not reveal how much we are hurting.

And foolishly, above all else, we believe this cycle will change without effort, and that a godly marriage is a guarantee from the day we say "I do."

We sadly and quite commonly have an illusive ideal of a godly marriage stuck in our heads that we are not actively working towards. Like a pretty picture hanging on a wall, we simply stare at it and admire it. We have plenty of nice thoughts about it, but we are not actually doing the work required to obtain it. Maybe the lies we have swallowed down have us convinced that we never can, that we never will.

Those types of marriages are for *other* people who are far more spiritual and much less flawed than we. *That* kind of marriage does not exist for *normal* people, who argue over where to eat dinner, where to put the keys, and how to fold the laundry. *Our* marriage has weathered one too many storms to ever look like *that*.

Do any of these lines sound familiar to you? They are proof of the toll this world and the enemy has taken on our marriages. Only through pursuing Christ, together and fervently, can we ever hope to change this picture.

The truth is, just because two believers get married, we are not guaranteed a godly, Christ-seeking, sacrificially-loving, sanctification-desiring covenant. It only means you have the opportunity to make one if you are willing to put in the work that is required. Thankfully it *does* guarantee that you do not fight alone towards making your marriage meaningful from an eternal standpoint. It allows our seemingly small efforts to be paired with a faithful God who can do immeasurably more in our marriages than we ever thought possible, as long as we invite Him into the brokenness.

To start the process of unlearning the lies and begin to make progress we must remember that we have been made worthy of love, second chances, and grace...

...and so has our spouse. We cannot obtain the radical

transformation of accepting the way that God views us without also changing the way we look at our husbands. The grace that is sufficient for us is more than enough to cover them, too.

In order to embrace this, it is going to take prayer and open conversation. Trust me, there will be some uncomfortable moments as our sin, pride, and flaws are exposed for our spouse to both see and hold us accountable to moving past. I mean, who really enjoys having their heart examined with a spiritual microscope? Not me. We do not enjoy owning up to our failures in the presence of God and our husbands. Our flesh just wants to be left alone, to do as it pleases without question. But take heart, this momentary discomfort pales in comparison to the joy of having a marriage where you are both on the same team, fighting for the same advancement of God's Kingdom.

Maybe for you this conversation starts with confessing the bitterness in your heart, in telling your husband about all of the struggles you have hidden away. Do not be surprised, offended, or take it personally when he comes back with struggles of his own. Consider it a status check on your spiritual lives as they stand, today. Let it be the starting point for your journey in unlearning, together.

Airing out these wounds and pent up anger can be so, incredibly difficult, and that is okay. Like any home renovation, it is going to get really messy before it gets really good. We must hold on to hope, trusting that our Foundation remains in tact, even as the surface level is torn to shreds. Do not forget that God is honored in our moments of vulnerability; He is honored in our sludge-hammered walls and the mess that ensues. He is waiting, patiently, to rebuild from the ground up, and something tells me His floor plan for marriage leaves a lot more room for grace.

Maybe you some of you have already started this process, and now that everything is out in the open, you feel overwhelmed. You cannot see a clear next step, and the task seems too daunting to undertake. Remember that you, the collective you, do not fight alone in this. God is with you in your moments of weakness, waiting to reveal His power and strength in the beautiful form of redemption. He wants order, not chaos, for your marriage. He does not delight in the discord of His children.

My encouragement to you in this place, whether you are just beginning the journey or are stuck waiting for a next step, is to go to the Cross. Literally, get on your knees with your husband and go to the Lord. Honestly, when was the last time you did so?

Ask Him what He wants to heal.
Surrender the heavy lifting to Him.
Trust that He longs to renew your minds as you press into restoration.

Since this marriage stuff is both hard work and a beautiful adventure, I like think of it as being in a kayak on the open waters. Someone has to sit in the front, and someone has to sit in the back. This does not mean the person in front is any more important, by the way, it just means that you each must have your own defined place—but it absolutely takes two people paddling equally as hard to get the kayak moving. And if you are going in different directions? You will spin in circles until your arms give out and you decide to call it quits.

I love to use this example because Taylor and I had an experience on a kayak in the open waters of the Gulf of Mexico. We'll just say our directional skills were seriously lacking, there was a salt water marina involved, and we bit off significantly more than we could chew. We ended up paddling into waters much deeper than we anticipated. This is true of our kayak trip in Florida, but also true of our marriage. We had no idea what we were really getting into. So yes, for us, marriage is like kayaking, and we still have much to learn about these waters we are navigating.

In a similar manner, divorces happen because we spend all of our efforts trying to get our marriages to *different* places. So when we wake up after twenty-five years and we have not moved an inch, we are ready to walk away because our efforts have been exhausted in failed attempts to move in opposite directions. Do not be the couple spinning in circles for twenty years because you cannot decide where you want to go. Do not spend all of your time on the shore because you refuse to sit in the back, or the front, or whatever place you think is most important.

Decide who needs to sit where, pick up your paddle, and get to work.

Questions for Unlearning

- How do I view my role in marriage?

- Do I base this on God's design for marriage, my family expectations, or the cultural mandates of womanhood?

- What has influenced my views of marriage in positive and negative ways?

- What have I learned from society, family, and church about marriage in my personal experience?

- How have these lessons shaped my thought life regarding marriage?

Additionally, for those of you who are already married:

- What unhealthy thoughts and habits could I really do without in my marriage?

- Do I operate in a striving manner, to avoid guilt and feelings of unworthiness, or do I operate out of love, sacrificially
serving my husband, as he does the same for me?

- How can I communicate this desire for renewed thinking to my spouse?

- What steps can I take towards understanding God's heart for me as a Christ-following woman first, and as a wife second?

Challenge Six

For the Mrs.

As uncomfortable as it may be, grab your spouse, because it's time to get them involved in this part of the process. Go over the questions for unlearning with them, and if they are willing, have them answer those questions for themselves, too. By discussing your current roles in marriage, and whether or not those seem to be working, you can create space to make adjustments if you both deem them necessary.

The next part of the challenge? Spend one night out this week at dinner, grabbing coffee, or splitting a bottle of your favorite wine, and have an honest conversation about where your marriage is now, and where you want it to go. Be sure to write out some concrete steps you can *both* take towards reaching your marriage goals.

Finally, spend time in prayer together, and for each other, every day for the next week. Commit to learning what your spouse most needs prayer for each day, and to do so regardless of any small disagreements or difficult conversations that may come up. Take notice of the things that change for the better as you spend more time praying for your spouse instead of dwelling on their perceived imperfections. Watch closely as the things you may normally argue about seem to pale in comparison to the desire to see your marriage become a place of encouragement and sanctification. I have a feeling you might just extend this challenge past the seven days I'm asking for, and I sincerely pray that you do!

For the Ms.

If you are headed down the aisle soon, go ahead and dive in to the above challenge. If you are currently living a life without a serious dating partner, my challenge to you is this: *enjoy it.*

Don't spend too much time dwelling on what could be, should be, or might one day be. Don't fall into the trap of waiting for marriage to allow yourself to really enjoy your life. You have a certain kind of freedom and mobility that your married friends don't, so take advantage of it! Pick your own movie. Eat wherever, and whatever, you want. Enjoy spending twenty bucks without having to run it by your spouse. Heck, take a last minute trip because you don't have to juggle multiple calendars. Whatever you choose, do something for yourself this week, and celebrate the joy it is to be single!

Let Us Pray

Lord, we thank you for the beautiful marriage relationship you have created. We thank you that you allow us to experience a glimpse of your sacrificial, humble love in the midst of our marriages as we learn to love like you do. We confess to you that our pride and selfishness get in the way of our loving our spouses the way you intended us to, and for that, we ask for your forgiveness. For those of us who are married, we ask that you renew our hearts to be full of humility and respect for the man you created for us. For those of us who are not, we ask you keep us from waiting until we are married to receive the joy you so freely offer us regardless of our relationship status. Wherever we are today, we admit that our love does not look like your love—but we want it to. We admit that we have looked to marriage to define us, even though we know it never truly can. We ask that you replace our desire to be served with a desire to serve; and the need for affirmation with the certainty of who you say we are, as believers first and as wives second. We trust that you can restore our ideas about marriage to be in line with the covenant relationship you intended, and we ask that you move in our hearts as we seek to redefine our roles within it.

Let's Talk About Sex

Take a deep breath, this chapter is not what you think.

This is not a lecture about abstinence; nor is it a filtered conversation about the birds and the bees. I will not pretend to be a holier-than-thou woman pointing a condemning finger at your tarnished past or one night stands or whatever it is that you have learned to call your unwise choices. This is a real life conversation about sex. I am not going to bother with a lengthy list of opinions as to why saving yourself for marriage is best, and if you're wondering why that is, you are not alone. When I first sat down to write this chapter, I completed it in its entirety without even thinking *once* of abstinence, and even I questioned my own silence on the issue.

So, why did I leave it out? I will just tell you honestly. I was not convicted or lead or otherwise prodded to approach the topic because this book is supposed to be for real, messy women with real, messy lives. If we were all sitting together in my living room talking about sex, I would not bring it up then, either. Why not? Well, chances are, the vast majority of you reading this have already had sex, and chances are, not all of you waited until marriage.

This leaves me with two options. I can either write an entire chapter that's going to heap guilt and shame onto your weary heart in a wasted attempt to break through to you, sure. I could do that. Many other books certainly have. Or, we can call it like we see it, and move forward. We can talk about the issues we *really* face as Christian women who have sex. We can talk about it openly, without pretending that it is so clean and simple--and that is okay. We have to get back to the basics of Who made sex, why He made it, and where we have gone so, incredibly wrong in the ways we've learned to think about it. This is where we will begin:

Sex is
1) Designed intentionally
2) by God
3) to be enjoyed

We have to come to grips with all three parts of this statement if we are ever going to engage in healthy, scripturally-based conversations about sex.

In order to do that, we must first admit that sex was designed with a purpose in mind. It is no mistake that it takes two, and it is no mistake that we enjoy it so much. God *specifically* made sex to be something we like, something amazing. After all, it *is* the act that He uses to create new life. It's kind of an incredible ordeal, and God is not removed from the equation, not in the slightest. He is right there in the midst of it, because yeah, God made sex and it is *good.*

In all likelihood, you have one of three gut reactions to the above statement. Your response to it will actually give a pretty clear picture of the mindset you were raised with. This reaction will reveal whether social or religious thought gripped your attention first on the matter, and where we should go from here.

1. "Lady, you are off your rocker. Why would you drag God into the conversation about s-e-x? What is *wrong* with you? S-e-x is like fight club—rule one is *never* talk about it. Next chapter, please."

2. "Well. Now that you mention it, that actually sounds about right. God did make Adam and Eve, and they did make babies. I guess sex is for enjoyment, too, right? You know, not that I do it or anything. Next chapter, please."

3. "I thought this book was supposed to be informative...what else was sex made for? This is not rocket science. Sex is good. Next chapter, please."

Well, we won't be skipping ahead to the next chapter just yet. If I have not lost you already, I will shed some light on the response you just gave, and tell you why it matters what you think about sex.

If your answer resembled the first response, it is likely you were raised in a conservative Christian environment. Accessories included a purity ring and true love waits t-shirt in your teen years, and you've been taught (whether explicitly or implicitly) that sex is one of those things you simply do not talk about. For you, feelings towards sex may include shame, guilt, anxiety, uncertainty, and confusion in regards to sexual desires. Should you already be married or have had your first sexual encounter, I am willing to bet you are lugging around some heavy baggage regarding your views on it. This weight does not have to remain on your shoulders. Maybe you were not taught how to talk or think or feel towards sex when you were young, but there is time and grace enough for you to learn some healthy habits and ways of understanding what God truly intends for us in our intimate relationships.

If your answer more closely resembled the second response, you may or may not have been raised in a Christian environment, but at some point, you entered into a relationship with Jesus Christ and have accepted that God and sex do, in fact, coexist. You were raised to understand that yes, sex is a part of life, but not necessarily a part of life as designed by God. You may have some reservations or confusions regarding what

God has to say about sexual relations, but you are open to learning. You may or may not have sported a purity ring in your teen years.

If your response is in alignment with the third opinion, I am willing to bet that you either a) did not grow up in an overtly Christian environment or b) had parents who were incredibly open about the realities we're surrounded with. In other words—you were not a sheltered child, so your parents gave you a healthy dose of reality. You may be the most open to talking about sex in general, but you also may have some patterns of thinking that do not fully comprehend all that God intends sex to be like.

Our first impressions regarding sexual relations are very important for us to grasp in terms of our own unlearning. Where, when, and how we first learn about sex becomes a psychological and physiological script that we follow from that moment forward. That is, however we first encounter sex will largely shape our thoughts on it, well into adulthood. This is seen true in cases of abuse, assault, and children or adolescents exposed to pornography at a young age. It is also seen in the average, everyday teen regarding their own sexual history and discovery. Thus the thoughts we form when we first encounter and experience sex can and will also shape the way we act on those impulses later in life.

Hint? This is *important*.

We must take notice of how sex first gripped our attention in our own lives before we seek to start this process of unlearning. For some of you, this brings back traumatic memories, and you are desperately hoping I will gloss over this sex topic quickly and superficially. This is because sex, too, has been used as a weapon against the hearts of men and women.

To those of you walking away from the chains of addiction, abuse, or utter confusion, my heart believes you will find healing. Know that Jesus *longs* to bring you that healing. I know that for some of you, this is the chapter you want to skip, because the memories that it triggers are terrifying and haunting all at the same time.

I feel lead, at the urging of the Holy Spirit, to speak specifically to you, friend. To those of you crawling out of sexual hell, I remind you that there are physiological responses that do not constitute consent. I remind you that when you say no, that is enough. You should not have to fight beyond that, so if you were unable to do so, let go of that guilt *right now* because your word should have been enough. To those of you walking away from a string of casual hookups, I remind you that you have been made a new creation in Christ and that the old you has passed away. To those of you who have turned to sex as way to self-medicate, I remind you that those mistakes and moments of weakness and times you turned to sex for comfort do not define you, nor do they do not detract value from you. Take heart in knowing that the men who have used you and mistreated you in the name of sex will have to answer for their actions. Be encouraged in the truth that your past does not eliminate the possibility of a healthy sexual relationship for you in the context of marriage later on.

For those of you who have suffered at the hands of someone who asserted more power over you than any one person should have, take comfort in knowing that you do not struggle alone. For those who question—unsure if what you endured constitutes abuse, unlearn here and now what our culture has taught you regarding the matter. No longer can we sit in silence and pretend that abuse only involves black eyes and girls who "ask for it". No longer can we blame the victim for the rape culture we are drowning in. No longer can we pretend that abuse does not have long-term psychological effects. No longer can we go on, acting as if it does not happen in our schools and churches and families—because for a third of you reading this book, this has been your reality, too. We have much to unlearn if we are ever going to truly live after having survived it.

So we must take all the junk that we have been told about abuse and bruises and not knowing our place. Dump it here. Leave it all here.

I am endlessly sorry that we have been taught to ask, "What was she wearing?" rather than, "Why couldn't he control himself?" I am sorry we have been taught to think, "She must have been drunk" and not, "He must have been stupid." I am sorry that we live in a culture that questions, "Why didn't she fight harder?" and not, "Why didn't he listen when she said no?" You are not alone in the struggle, and God has not forgotten you.

Know that regardless of your past, He intends for you to experience sex the way it was designed to be—and there will be a holy moment of restoration in your heart when you do. There is still hope. There is *always* hope, because for every ounce of guilt that we bring to the foot of the cross; there is an ocean of grace to swallow it up. For every drop of your shame, there is healing in the blood shed for you. Redemption is your reality, because God no longer sees you for your sin. If you have struggled in this area and doubt that you have been forgiven, know that God still loves you beyond measure, and has made you *completely* and *totally* clean.

The reason this can be so hard to accept, and the cause of our awkward struggle, is the potency of sex on our physical bodies. Neurologically speaking, sex activates strong and stubborn stimulants in our brains. Maslow's Hierarchy of Needs even goes as far as to classify sex in the same category of human essentials such as food, water, and breathing. The sexual urges we feel are evidenced to be as strong as the desire to find water after a grueling ten-mile hike. This unfortunately makes it more difficult to rewire our thought life on the matter than a host of other things, but it is not impossible. Much like any other drug, our bodies and brains can become addicted to the cravings of intimacy, but a little rehabilitation can undo the damage.

The issue when we not learn how to talk about sex, is that all of our good intentions and "true love waits" promises tend to fly out the window as we fall into our serotonin and dopamine induced comas. This certainly has the ability to cloud our judgment and make for some rather intricate emotional entanglements. The haze of physical affection often puts the biblical wisdom we know on the back burner as we try to blindly navigate the minefield of our physical desires.

So when we add in our feelings of guilt and shame, as we are often lead to by the teachings in our religious circles, this mess only grows. It is okay if you are unsure how to think or feel about sex, many believers are, and many non-believers are, too. The lies we have come to accept as truth regarding sex, paired with the physical and emotional weight it carries, make for some heavy and confusing burdens. So not only are we seemingly left to fend for ourselves in terms of the strongest impulses known to humankind, but this is also the topic we are least educated on in our churches.

Something seems wrong with this picture, because the art of sex that God had in mind when He created us looks nothing like what I see around me. We are flooded with sexual expectations. Truly and completely, we have been inundated with lies and false realities and bad jokes about what our broken world deems acceptable in terms of sex. Our culture says "doing the dirty" is nothing more than a pawn in our modern day chess game we call dating, and that scares me. Self-gratification has become the ultimate idol, and its favorite game is convincing us that sex is king. The lust of the flesh is the most insatiable of beasts, and we feed it daily with pornography, casual hookups, romance novels, and whatever else we use to scratch the itch of our sexual addictions. Don't believe me? Let's look at some numbers.

- The average age of first sexual encounter is 17.
- An estimated 50% of internet use is associated with sex.
- In a recent study, one fourth of men that participated admitted to viewing pornography online in the 30 days prior to the questionnaire.
- One tenth of women admitted to doing the same.

This dangerous mentality tells us, if it feels good, we should do it, regardless of the outcome or the implications it has for the human right to be treated with dignity. It says that satisfying your sexual desires is an acceptable and understandable goal, but know that this directly counters every caution regarding sex we are given in the New Testament.

I get that these ideas about sex in our heads sex are harshly and deeply ingrained. It is likely that you started learning various sexual scripts as early as the age of six or seven, based on what you saw at home, watched on television and the things you heard from your peers in school. This occurs in both processes of primary and secondary socialization we discussed earlier, as societal pressures largely impact our views on sexual interactions.

What starts as cooties and k-i-s-s-i-n-g in elementary school quickly grows into the animal of comparison, the weight of peer pressure, and an increased awareness of social scripts regarding our sexual involvements. These scripts dictate what is acceptable and not acceptable in terms of romantic relationships and physically intimate contact. We may playfully call these scripts things like "the bro code," the "three date rule", or "the walk of shame," but the truth they reveal about our views on sex are anything but fun.

For women in particular, this set of cultural demands about when and how we engage in sexual relations are widely acknowledged as valid societal rules that we ought to follow. And if you're fighting to avoid sex altogether, such rules can make this seem like an old-fashioned and impossible goal. So, what do these expectations look like, and what can we do to refute them?

For one, there is an understanding that at a certain point, be it a fifth date or a hundred-dollar steak or a round of margaritas, sex is *owed.* No longer is it a question of "if" someone will engage in casual sex, but rather we are left to decide, "when" it is most appealing to us. The expectation, now, is that women will *eventually* "put out" under the right set of circumstances. This leaves men waiting for their romantic efforts to be requited with physical intimacy, and women feeling guilty if they do not engage in the societal ritual. I mean, he *did* spend all day planning that romantic picnic in the park, right? Doesn't he deserve a little *somethin'-somethin'*? (Just to clarify, sex is a gift meant to be shared freely in the context of biblical romance, it is *never* owed as a form of "payment.")

Secondly, when we dig deeper, we see the dual expectation that women must somehow both maintain our sexual innocence, and be wildly experienced at the same time. A lady on the street, but a freak in the sheets, anyone? We must play both the whore and the virgin in this dichotomy, and the confusion these conflicting roles bring can be devastating as men are taught to desire this impossible fantasy. We see this in magazines, where women are dressed like overtly sexualized school girls, desperately in need of being "taught a few lessons." We also see this evidenced in sitcoms where the handsome male lead wants nothing more than to deflower the wildly attractive and somehow kinky virgin. These situations may seem trivial, but their very existence reveals to us that our culture's views on sex are far from what God had in mind when he made Adam and Eve. So it now falls to us to refute the ultimate lie about sex that has captured our society—not only that our physical desires reign above all else, but also that they are without consequence.

Sex, being something that our Creator intended to be both free and a representation of freedom, has been marred into something that can be bought and sold as easily as any other commodity. The horrifying truth? Men are addicted to the bodies of our young sisters. Women are addicted to the lie that sex will validate their existence. And we are all addicted to the most dangerous lie of all: that it is simply not a big deal; that we do not need to step in. This is where I start to get nauseas. Our culture claims, loudly, that sex is for everyone, the Bible says sex is for your only one. Feeding our desires has become the highest goal, leaving emotions and healthy relationships to rot in the past like forgotten relics of ancient history.

As long as no one accidentally gets pregnant, it doesn't matter what happens, right?
As long as she's into it, it's okay if it hurts, yeah?
I know he's married, but it's fine if he really loves me, isn't it?

In a word? No.
I'll call that what it is--fifty shades of crap.

We have some work to do, because when I look at the upcoming generation, I shudder to think of what their moldable minds are being taught about sex. Between their peers and television and what they see online, I guarantee you this: they are learning about sex everywhere *except* for the church or at home. They will turn to Cosmopolitan magazine for the latest sex tips long before they open up the Bible to see the romance God intends to accompany it. Doesn't that worry you, just a little? Isn't it scary to know that in a generation of selfies and Instagram filters, young girls are also being taught how to "sext"? How to Tinder? How to SnapChat nude pictures?

Like everything else in this upcoming generation, sex is becoming instantly obtainable. You can broadcast your body as easily as you can update a Facebook status. So for those of you who who feel our silence is acceptable, I propose that we need to get our side of this conversation started before our culture finishes it for us. We absolutely must teach our young ones about the Garden of Eden sex that God created before anyone else steps in and uses it as a weapon against their young hearts.

The choice we have, the crucial decision, is to either remain silent—or to join in the conversation. We have the opportunity to offer wise counsel; to talk about the reality of sex and its consequences, both the good and bad; the emotional and the physical.

So where is the hint that says this stuff is important? We are told in scripture countless times to stay away from sexual immorality—because this war is not a new one. This struggle echoes as far back as the Bible itself. As Christ followers, we have a responsibility to start looking at this part of our lives critically and through the lens of the scriptures.

This kind of conversation is essential for us to have because the enemy clearly uses sex, too. What God intended to be a worshipful act of freedom, he has turned for some into a hellacious realm of bondage. We see this manifest itself in pornography addictions, extramarital affairs, and the broken marriages they cause. We see the evidence of this war on the faces of sex slaves down the street and across the country. Prostitution, strip clubs, and child sex tourism thrive at the hands of the enemy and his destruction of sexual relations. It is enough to turn my stomach, and let us be clear: this should turn our stomachs. This should challenge us to work towards a renewed understanding of the holy act of worship sex was meant to be.

That is why we must unlearn the habits about sex that our society is cramming into our heads and get back to the heart of what God made sex to look like. In a day and age where social media has become the laugh track to our sitcom-esque lives; we must recognize that sex and abuse and pornography are not laughing matters. Every time a joke is made at the expense of pornography, it is really made at the expense of the likely underage girl seduced by the sex industry into producing it. I know, this stuff is heavy. I have been told to lighten up about the subject; to that I say, sober up and get over yourself. This is no laughing matter.

The lives of teenage girls being forced to sell their bodies to feed the sexual urges of the well-to-do men in our country is no laughing matter. Child sex tourism largely sustained by American men is no laughing matter. Child rape is no laughing matter. We must unlearn our humor if we find this funny. We better get on our knees to pray for a change of heart is this is what we deem comedic. As Christ followers, we cannot allow this to fly under the radar anymore, nor can we turn a blind eye. We have an obligation to reclaim the sanctity of sex within marriage and take the rest of the believers with us on our journey.

Where do we go from here?
What can we do?
What should we do?
Where did we go wrong?

The truth is, the moment we as humankind felt the need to cover ourselves with leaves in the garden, sex has been anything but simple.

The church has some very important things to say about sex. (Or at least they would if they ever talked about it.) The conversation usually goes a little something like this, "You absolutely should not have sex outside of marriage. This is what the Bible says."

...and that is the full extent of our spiritual sex-ed.

Wait, what?

Yes, *this* is the awkward conversation we have created with our hush-hush mentality. I'd say the silent treatment isn't going so well, yeah?

The mindset currently adding to this problem? Should you want to talk about how a woman experiences sex in our culture, you have to automatically be a feminist. Apparently talking about a woman's sexuality somehow has become synonymous with empowerment. And according to the silence emanating from our pulpits, if you are talking about women's sexuality or *any* sexuality for that matter, you must not be a Christian, so you'd better keep your mouth shut.

We must rewrite that religious-societal script if we ever hope to have the Church to weigh in on honest and constructive conversations about sex. As of now, women cannot talk about it, adolescents do not learn truth about it, and everyone at church pretends not to do it. I call Bologna Sandwich on the whole shebang, ya feel me?

It is high time we admit that our silence has only added to the problem and perversion of something intended to be so holy and beautiful. The time where we remain silent and inactive about the education regarding this matter is over. If we stay quiet now, we are passively supporting the sex-obsessed culture that surrounds us. We cannot conform, and we cannot ignore it. This is the time and place for the church to step up to the plate for Christianity and our beliefs on sexual relations.

So, why don't we hear sermons about s-e-x on Sunday morning?

Perhaps we deem it too messy; we think it is none of our business. Maybe the harsh reality is that we simply would not know what to say if we opened our mouths to speak. I think this silence reveals the deeper issue; the root of the problem. We do not talk about sex because we have not sought out God's design for it, and we are terrified by our culture's definition of it. Instead, we sit quietly and awkwardly in our pews, as we hoard our questions and confusion. We allow society to steer the conversation because we feel that we have nothing to contribute. Surely Christians cannot say anything about sex aside from teaching abstinence, right?

Wrong. We can, and we should.

This has weighed increasingly heavy on my heart because in a few short weeks, I will be welcoming a son of my own into the world. My blood pressure already skyrockets when I think about the war that will be waged on his young mind, using the bodies of women as ammunition. My husband and I are already anticipating that he will be flooded with ideas and lies about sex at an incredibly young age, and that scares us. I tell you truly, I would much rather have the difficult birds and bees conversations with our son at home, then to face his scars and wounds in the aftermath of the sexually charged culture being forced on the minds of our young ones. The discomfort of prevention far outweighs the cost of the cure.

So, it is time to bring this all together if we are earnest about breaking the silence. Simply put: We cannot impart wisdom that we do not have. We cannot teach positive, healthy ways to talk about sex if we still stumble awkwardly through the dialogue. We have to unlearn our *own* flawed thinking about sexual relations first. We have to open our hearts before we open our mouths. We turn to the Word, and we hold on to hope.

I do not have all of the answers, but what I do know is this— God intended sex to be beautiful, holy, and sacred. It is meant to be a place of freedom and vulnerability, not marred by fear or judgment. I know what our culture says and I get that the prognosis is grim. It is easy to see that chivalry is a lifeless corpse we are desperately trying to revive. I am trackin', trust me...

...but even so, I want this to soak into your soul if you will let it. Just one, summative truth of God's intentions for sex: It was created to be a good thing.

The scene we find ourselves reading about in Song of Solomon is based around a relationship before, during, and after the wedding night. The language used was so romantic and even deemed provocative enough that Jewish men were encouraged to abstain from reading certain portions of the text until they reached their thirties.

What?

That's right. The Bible talks about sex, and so should we. The text is long and poetic, and so full of imagery that I encourage you to read the entire book on your own when you have the time. Even a brief excerpt would take up several pages here, so I will simply give you the summative notes instead. *(You're welcome.)*

The picture painted in this book is a journey through a romantic relationship, wedding, and honeymoon. Let's remember this; it is in the Bible for good reason. This is a divinely inspired handbook on how to pursue a lover. We find it in scripture because the heart of God is not removed from sex and romance—His heart is right in the midst of it. He literally inspired a book on sex to give us a glimpse of what He had in mind when He created us. This is important to Him, and it should be important to us, too. While we look into this, you will notice both the man and the woman are romanced and pursued on the wedding night, because the marriage bed is a place to want each other without reservation.

When we get into the passages about sex in this portion of the Bible, the language can seem maybe slightly *too* flowery for us to easily dissect. However, God's heart towards romance is clear to see, and *these* are the truths we can take away with confidence:

Divine romance is intentional and pursuant.
Divine romance accompanies the wedding night and the remainder of the marriage.

Divine romance is not separated from sex, but rather is all up in the midst of it.
Divine romance is okay with desiring your spouse intimately, both physically and emotionally.

In modern terms? God is for romance. He created it. He is for flowers and holding hands. He is for late night talks where you spill your heart out to a guy for the first time because you finally feel safe enough to do so. He is for opening doors and first dates at a coffee shop. He is for slow dances and the moment you feel like someone might actually love you the way you'd always hoped and dreamed they would. He is for redeeming the parts of you that were marred by the lies of worldly sex. He is for holy moments of reconciliation when you experience sex as He intended it to be. He is for sandy-footed, sun-kissed honeymoons and blissful days spent in bed because you're married and that's what you want to do. He is for sex. He is for love. He is for marriage. He is for romance. He is the author of love, and He designed it to be so, incredibly good.

The marriage bed is not meant to be a place of guilt. What, like it's a *bad* thing to enjoy sex with your husband? No, no. It is something we are biologically *programmed* to know how to do. Plain and simple: God could have made the baby-making process a lot less *fun*, but He *didn't*. It is a part of our nature. We were created with a deep longing to express intimate and passionate love. We were made to want our spouses and enjoy them physically, and that is *nothing* to be ashamed of. Enjoying sex is not a sin, not even close! By the way--talking about sex is not a sin, either, despite what the lens of religion may currently show you.

We must admit that sex is both a part of our culture and a part of God's design for us. We must define it as the Bible does and treat it with due diligence. If we continue to be too embarrassed to talk about it, the generations to come will not hear our voices on the matter—they will hear only what our broken world has to say, and that's not the picture of sex I want them to see first.

We have to come to terms with how sex has impacted our lives—good, bad, or ugly, and accept the grace God showers on us so we can move past it. It may seem as though the hard part is up to you, to surrender these beliefs and ideas to the Lord, but I promise He will do the heavy lifting of removing these burdens from your heart.

If you are still waiting to have sex until marriage, congratulations. It is no small feat to tame the emotional-physical impulses we are hard wired to have. Be thankful you have not *"awakened love before its time"*, and press on in your desire to wait until your wedding night. If, however, you have not waited until marriage, do not let your past discourage you into thinking you are unworthy of a Godly marriage, or that you have somehow disqualified yourself from sex as God intended it to be. Mistakes are real, and so is redemption, got it? There is grace enough and time to spare for you to unlearn the habits you have acquired so far, and there will be some incredible moments of freedom when you surrender those flawed beliefs and the burdens of your past to the Lord. Finally, for those of you who are already married, what are you waiting for?

Questions for Unlearning

- What do my initial responses to conversations about sex reveal about my thoughts towards it?

- What role has sex played in my life—good or bad?

- Am I feeling convicted in any way to change my thought life about sex, and why?

- If sex has been used as a weapon against me, through addiction or abuse or something else all-together, what steps towards healing can I take today?

- Do I typically follow along with our culture and its views of sex, or am I basing my thoughts, and therefore actions, on God's intention of romance?

- What can I glean from God's heart towards sex to help re-shape my patterns of thinking?

Challenge Seven

For this challenge, you will need to grab some paper and a pen, and set aside ample time to invest in untangling your ideas about sex as it pertains to you. Whether you are married, single, waiting until your wedding night, or that ship has already sailed, there is something for you, here.

All the single ladies and for those of you who are dating:

Just because you aren't in a marriage relationship now, doesn't mean that ideas about sex are magically absent from your life. Whether you've already had sex, or are waiting until marriage, chances are, at some point you will need to have a conversation with a significant other or potential spouse about your views on sex, and your sexual history if you have one. Your challenge is to figure out what to say if and when that time comes. If this includes sharing your goal to wait to have sex until you are married, be prepared to explain why this is important to you, and consider how you might respond if your partner has already engaged in sexual relations prior to meeting you. If this includes sharing about your own sexual history, be sure to view yourself through the eyes of grace.

If you are currently struggling with patterns of physical intimacy, or engaging in sexual relationships with a casual attitude, I challenge you to look honestly at why you are pursuing these physical encounters. Find someone, preferably a fellow Christ follower who you trust, to hold you accountable to answering these questions:

- Is sex really fulfilling you, or are you trying to fill a void left by pain?

- Are you looking for validation in men because you don't understand how God can bring you a complete identity?

- What habits are contributing to your current mentality about sex, and how can you change them?

Please know that anything holding you back from receiving forgiveness for those moments of weakness *can* be released, and you *can* be confident in the healing offered to you by Christ.

For the married folks

Seriously, what are you waiting for? Grab your husband and get busy!

Let Us Pray

Lord, we come to you, thankful for the beautiful ways you designed us to demonstrate love. We thank you for making sex to be something that pleases you, and brings joy to us as well. We confess that our views regarding sex, and maybe our own sexual history, isn't quite what you intended for us. We believe that the forgiveness you offer for our sexual pasts is real, and that we can choose to start fresh as you renew our thinking about what sex is meant to be. We ask that you burden our hearts to see sex as you intended it, and that we would be increasingly aware of the flawed thoughts our society imposes on us about what is acceptable in physical relationships. We ask for the courage to speak truth into the darkest places where sex is used as a weapon, and to do so even in our Christian communities. We ask that you open our eyes to see not only the ways the enemy uses sex against our generation, but also give us the desire and ability to counter the assault, to be a voice of reason. We ask that you renew our hearts in the places damaged by worldly sex and the lies it has told us, and that we would boldly accept the healing you offer freely to us. We believe that you are a loving Father, and that you desire for sex to be an act of worship in our lives. We ask that you remove any hindrances, false beliefs, old pain, or bad habits that keep it from being just that. We trust in the authority given to us over our earthly bodies as daughters empowered by your Spirit, and we ask for wisdom as we seek to undo the damage, both in our lives, and in the lives of women around us.

Pain & Other Hard Things

Let's get right down to it: we do not like to talk about our pain. We much prefer to gloss over hardships with generic phrases like, "a difficult season", "a temporary storm" or "a current struggle." We do not like to call our pain by its real name. We would much rather sit silently in our churches and pretend all is well. As long as no one asks us to raise our hand, stand up, and tell the *real* version of our testimony, we'll be just fine.

Maybe it is time to admit that what we are doing now, simply is not working. If we cannot call our pain by name, or understand how God intends to use it for our good, how are we supposed to move past it? We will not receive healing until we acknowledge and surrender what has been broken.

For some of us, It is as if we are going before the Ultimate Physician, grasping our open wounds, pretending that we are in perfect health as we bleed through our bandages. If we are not ready tell Him what hurts, we are not ready for it to be fixed. *This* is why we have to unlearn how we manage our pain.

So, what *exactly* is stopping us? The various lies we believe about pain have warped our thinking immensely. Our pain plays an important albeit uncomfortable role, and we must view it through fresh eyes if we hope to alter our understanding of the hardships we have endured thus far.

The first reason we have often failed to openly acknowledge the presence or depth of our pain, is that we have believed somewhere in our misguided hearts that we, as Christ followers, should never hurt deeply. It's like our wires got crossed and we learned to equate following Christ with easy living. Though this notion sounds comforting, it could not be further from the truth. The very essence of Jesus, His compassion, meant that He suffered *with us* in our brokenness, our humanness, our filth, our tears, and in even our physical pain. He suffered *fully* and was no stranger to earthly pain; neither were those who most closely followed Him. His disciples were jailed, beaten, beheaded, and even crucified for the sake of following Him. How did we get to believe Christ followers are meant to live pain-free lives? This is simply not the case, nor is this is reflected in the Word.

This lie that our salvation constitutes the absence and negates the impact of pain can burrow its way deeply into our hearts. This lie is the reason we feel justified in becoming angry with God when things start to unravel, when life starts to hurt. This is the reason we cry out, "Why me, Lord?" and not, "All for Your glory." The falsehoods we believe about pain are the reasons we hold on to useless and unbiblical clichés like, "God will never give me more than I can handle." Yes, He will and yes, He does. You and I both know better.

The presence of pain is depicted both in scripture and in the narrative of our own lives. So let us embrace this new truth that is evidenced in reality: following Jesus does not grant us immunity from seasons of deep, unrelenting pain. On the contrary, following Him actually *guarantees* it--but, and this is an important but, we are also promised that in that pain, we do not suffer alone. We are assured that we do not suffer without bearing fruit. We certainly do not suffer because the Lord has deemed us worthy of harm or deserving of retribution.

Our God is not an ant bully with a magnifying glass, looking for ways to torture us mere humans. If we view Him this way, we have equated pain with punishment, and largely misunderstood its purpose in our lives. We are told in scripture that Just as gold is refined through the flames, so we must too, be cleaned and made pure. Sometimes that burns like hell, but we come out solid *gold*.

Perhaps our approach regarding pain should be a lot less about "why," as we are not always given an answer, and a lot more about "what now," as we *are* promised that through our suffering, we gain patience, perseverance, and a hope that does not disappoint. The Lord, in His grace, allows pain to be used in building our faith. Truthfully, we rarely get to know why bad things happen. We have questions about our pain that cannot or will not be answered on this side of eternity. We may not always get dealt what looks like a good hand, but *we know that we know that we know*, our God is able and willing to redeem even the deepest of hurts, and He wants to use them to draw others into His plan of redemption.

The crucial choice, however, will always remain with us. We can choose to be angry; we can hold on to bitterness. These are the things our human nature prefers to do. Like a sore in your mouth you can't leave alone, we like to be reminded we are validated in our pain, that we are allowed to feel hurt.

Alternatively, we can allow the pain to bear fruit as we draw closer to the God Who is waiting to heal us. We can allow it to be repurposed as an Ebenezer of God's strength when He overcomes the unthinkable for us. We can boldly declare to those watching that yes, even in the midst of the flames, our God is *still* good. We can surrender the pain to His capable hands and trust that something beautiful *will come* out of these ashes.

Since we are crucially aware that pain is a part of our reality, we better figure out what to do with it. This is why we must take the terrifying but necessary first step of naming and acknowledging our pain. I know what you may be thinking.

"It must be easy for you to sit in your cozy office and write these words. Obviously, you have never dealt with real pain before.

Obviously, you do not know what I have been through."

You are absolutely right. I may not know your story, but I do know mine. That is why I tell you in earnest, I have wept and prayed over these words, as I reflect on the pain our Redeemer has carried me—kicking and screaming—out of. I write this because I know what it is like to sit in a church building, surrounded by believers, in the middle of dark times, when no one seemed to notice or care or acknowledge that someone in the congregation may actually struggle with something *real* and really *hard*.

I wrote this chapter out of desperate hope, because my heart longs for churches to be a *viable* and *safe* place for people turn to when they have suicidal thoughts. When they get raped. When their partner hits them for the first, or last, time. When the divorce papers are drawn up. When the other woman wins. When the baby's heart stops beating. When the stable job bottoms out. When the bills can't be paid. When the drinking becomes an addiction. When the child you raised becomes someone you don't recognize. When the panic attacks seem to take over your life.

In order to get to that place, we have some hard work to do. *This* is why we must learn how to talk about our pain, then identify the lies that pain has told us so that our understanding of it can be restored. I will go first.

My hurt has gone by many names, as I'm sure yours has, too. Early on in life, it was the drunken, deadbeat, "father" that was never in the picture. Later on into adulthood, it grew into the wounds I endured from trying to fill the void that he left with shallow relationships as I chased approval. Eventually, it culminated into a controlling and manipulative relationship that left me running on empty and doubting that God's grace was big enough to cover my mess.

Still carrying around the emotional baggage of my anxiety-filled childhood, I went off to college and joined one of the nation's largest ROTC programs at the age of 16. What I anticipated to be a fresh start, and the beginning of a grand adventure, turned out to be a lot more like hard work, sleepless nights, and resentment towards the Lord because He had the *nerve* to let my life be really stinking hard...*again*. All of my old hurts and questions about identity did not magically disappear the moment I stepped foot on campus as I had anticipated, and the presence of my unresolved pain became glaringly obvious. I wanted *nothing* to do with the pain, so I stashed it away like last year's Halloween candy and pretended all was well.

Once I set my mind on blaming God for my hardships, instead of allowing Him to grow my faith through them, things unraveled quickly like a snag on my favorite sweater. What I once deemed a solid foundation crumbled like sand beneath my combat boots as my Bible collected dust and my prayer life dwindled to nothing. When we view our pain as a direct attack from the Lord, our pride screams that we must dig our heels in and fight harder, that we must handle the pain and confusion on our own. So we convince ourselves that we do not need God to step in. I cannot speak for you, but that rarely turns out well for me.

One of the lies pain loves to tell, that I believed during this time, is that no one else *really* cares if we are hurting. We simply need to put on our brave face, power through, and in the process of convincing everyone else that we're fine, we lie to ourselves, too. No matter how big or small, when we pretend our unresolved pain has magically evaporated into thin air, our relationship with the Lord will be superficial, our faith will become stagnant, and the infection in our hearts will only continue to grow unchallenged and untreated.

When we fail to acknowledge or surrender our pain, as we try to hold together the broken pieces on our own, we will turn to surface level comforts seeking distraction, instead of running to the Lord to seek healing. It is, after all, a heck of a lot easier to continue numbing your mind with momentary diversions than it is to spend time before the throne in spiritual open heart surgery. You see, that's the thing about temporal relief—it does not require that we explain ourselves, air our dirty laundry, or expose our hidden tears. It serves only our flesh as we seek to perfect our masks of independence. It reinforces the lie that we are fine just as we are, and that we do not need any help. Because the fix we get from our emotional band-aids is only temporary, we will continually search in all of the wrong places for new ways to validate our pain, appease our flesh, and ignore the symptoms of the growing abscess in our hearts. And so our pain convinces us we are no longer in need of a Savior during the very moments we most need Him.

For me, managing my pain was all about pride, that I could handle it on my own, and validation, that I was justified in my anger towards God. I desperately needed to hear I was still physically attractive—what I thought of as beautiful at the time—despite the bulky uniform and sunken eyes from lack of sleep. My pain made me crave physical, immediate, and tangible comfort based on a flesh-driven need for approval. I needed to know that someone saw something in me—anyone, anything would do. So it did. He was handsome and suave with a killer smile, and he seemed harmless...enough.

He was 23. *Red flag number one.*
A senior, no less. *Red flag number two.*
He never wanted me to meet his friends, take me to dinner, or spend time in a group. *Red flag number three.*

Pain can make us do desperate things as we search for our next five-minute fix to find relief.

In my reality, I was lonely, angry, and unwilling to turn to the Lord for rescue from the isolation. It was far more appealing to live a life of unchallenged sin than to do the hard work of letting him heal me, even if that meant getting further hurt in the process. *Finally,* I thought, *someone who does not expect me to act like the Christian woman I know I am called to be. Someone who will not call me out on my sin; who will cater to my flesh and tell me how pretty I look in my little black dress while I take tequila shots and make questionable choices.* That's how every good and healthy relationship begins, right? Right.

Little did I know that he too, was hurting, and looking for someone to hurt. Like many sources of our pain, he was not what he originally appeared to be. He could sense that I was young and naïve; that I was desperate for attention and approval. On the inside, if I were being honest, I would have admitted that I felt alone, broken, and in desperate need of validation. Instead of speaking the truth and paying attention to the warning signs, I blindly played the overly-confident, party-hard college gal that nothing and no one could ever hurt. So when he swooped in looking like a real life prince charming, I figured he was as good as any other distraction from my pain. He may as well have showed up with my missing glass slipper and a few talking mice, but our ending turned out to be anything but happily ever after.

Like an emotional narcotic, I became addicted to the distraction he provided for me. He managed to somehow falsely comfort me in my pain while simultaneously adding to it. I hated him and craved his attention all at the same time. He treated me like an *object* to be used at his leisure, and my identity hinged on his fleeting approval. No longer did I turn the pages of my Bible for truth or assurance of the Lord's goodness. No longer did I pray to the God I so strongly believed I would follow to the end of my days. My world had shifted, and the Lord was no longer in the center of it.

I became so accustomed to the pain I was ineffectively managing, I had *no idea* how heavy the burden had really become. I opted to numb this pain with temporary highs and the ultimate lie that I was living an "independent" and "empowered" life by self-medicating with this toxic relationship. It's like I was trying to soothe an emotional paper cut with a dirty band aid. Sure, It was effective for a short time, but the wound would never heal. And still, I refused to acknowledge or accept the pain. I was fine, really. Until I wasn't.

The slope called pain is slippery, dear friend. A once-passionate advocate for respect within dating relationships, I sat on the floor of my college dorm room, finally coming to grips with my reality.

For all of my feigned independence, He controlled me.
He had isolated me away from friends, family, and anyone who might suspect that something wasn't quite healthy.
I had not prayed, really prayed, in months.
My Bible sat unopened on my bookcase as I chased after his approval.
I found my identity solely in how I looked while I shallowly pursued earthly validation.
I turned to people, seeking comfort, and came up empty handed.
I lived in the house my pain had built me, and I felt that I would never escape.

All the while, my hurt was telling my exquisite lies and elaborate stories to keep me quiet and immobile. These things I learned from this man, who claimed to love me? They distorted my thinking, because that is how pain operates. It leads to false beliefs about ourselves that can take years of hard work to unlearn. I accepted the lie that I was nothing more than damaged goods. I thought that no one would ever, I do mean ever, want to marry me—certainly not the Godly kind of man I had always dreamed of, anyways. The way I saw it? I should hold on to whatever and whoever I could get—because no one else was going to want to love me through my mess.

Even more so, all the dreams I had of ministering to women and reaching people for God's Kingdom seemed to slip through my hands. The infection had spread far and wide, to the point that I believed that I was too far gone for Jesus and His grace—and was certainly too damaged to *ever* be used in a place of ministry. Who would listen to *me*, a rebellious *sinner* with a messy life? I was convinced there was *no way* Jesus could love me through the filth. Like a white dress covered in red wine stains, I believed there was no way I would ever be clean again. That is what pain does. It keeps our vision narrowly focused, limiting our foresight to the next labored step. It renders us unable to think beyond the current moment. This is why I couldn't see the story God was writing on my heart. I didn't know the depth and totality of redemption that awaited me. But God knew, and all the while I was running from Him, He was busy planning my rescue.

The eventuality of pain is this: it demands to be felt. Each of us has a tipping point where we must admit that we are broken, no matter how hard we fight to pretend that it is not so. Our pride wants desperately for us to resist any effort towards healing. It tells us to ignore that whisper of hope in our hearts that says there is a way out of this darkness...

...but no matter how hard and fast we run, our pain will catch up with us. So on a Tuesday night somewhere around three AM, I let the levy break. I finally acknowledged my pain before the Lord, and oh, did it hurt.

Even in that moment, when my pride told me I was at my weakest, I felt a comforting, strengthening presence unlike any other I had experienced or encountered. That whisper of hope was now loud and clear, calling me back to the Savior I had pushed away with all my might. This call that beckoned to me sounded a lot like grace; the kind that could cover my sins a thousand times over. The kind of redemption I thought was eternally out of my reach was holding me together on the cold tile floor.

I was in the very presence of the *Great I Am*. My limbs, tired from running, knelt under the weight of His glory. But this weight did not crush me—it surrounded me; it carried me to the foot of the Cross. So I did the only thing I could do.

I fell to my knees and I cried out. From the depths of my soul, I cried out to the Lord. I shouted at Him. I plead with Him. My heart begged for mercy while my pain questioned His goodness. I was angry to realize the depth of what I had endured. I was bitter, as I could not understand why God had allowed me to hurt in this way. The infection of pain had rendered me unable to see the protection and provision He was for me even while I pushed Him away like a rebellious bride wandering through a desert. *How could a good, loving God allow me to hurt like this?* I spat out such bitter words—I left no hurt unspoken, no accusation unstated. And when I finally ran out of things to say, I rested there in the silence. I had wrestled with God; I had said my piece.

Before the throne, where I expected the wrath of His judgment, I was surrounded with His compassion. Where I anticipated condemnation, I was met with grace. All of the punishment I thought awaited me at the feet of Jesus? He took it for me in the form of the nails in His hands and feet. In the spear in His side. In the crown of thorns He wore for me. In the tomb He inhabited for me. In the death He died for me. He did not only suffer *with* me in my pain, He also suffered *for* me that I might be rescued out it.

...and then He spoke.
This is where my story *really* begins.
"Daughter, don't you know that I still love you?
Don't you know that you are carrying pain I never intended you to handle on your own?
Give it up—give up the burden.
I don't want you to live with this pain.
I still have a purpose for you, I will still use you for my Kingdom.
But you have to *get up* out of this pit.
I say to you, Daughter, rise up!"

...and then all at once, the chains on my heart were broken.
I felt the words as if they were spoken into my ear, like a secret between closest friends.
I felt the weight physically leave my body, as if sandbags had been removed from my weary shoulders.
I felt life come back into my veins.
It all flooded back, like waking up from a spiritual coma.
I was alive.
I was *free*.

I will not tell you that this road back to the Lord has been an easy one. I will not tell you that I never looked back, never faltered, never again struggled or questioned or shouted. I will tell you that like Jacob, I have wrestled with God—and He gave me a new name. He is waiting to reclaim you, too; longing to repurpose your pain.

What the enemy once declared as our broken identities, the Lord will restore into beauty. Like the sick woman who had been bleeding for twelve years, He calls us *daughter* and gives our life a new significance far beyond the pain we feel. He takes the time to hear our story in its entirety and heals us of our seemingly incurable diseases.

That is our identity, but our pain tells us some elaborate stories to make us think otherwise. Tell me, friend, what lies has your pain told you?

If you feel you are to blame for the suffering you have endured, you may believe that you allowed it, or could have prevented it *if only you had done _____*. That is what pain does; it makes us hate the parts of ourselves that were weak enough to get hurt. If you feel that your pain has disqualified you from being used in a place of ministry, you might falsely equate your pain with punishment for a sin that you continue to grasp guilt over. If you do not believe you can be fully healed, your pain has likely taught you to either doubt that God wants to heal you, or even more dangerously so, that He is unable to do so. These are dirty lies from a sneaky enemy who preys on our brokenness.

Please do not make the mistake, as I did, of allowing this pain to consume your existence as a whole. It will only further warp your thinking and your view of the God who is longing to journey with you towards healing.

The lie of pain as identity makes us lash out against our Abba Father, the One who is waiting all along to heal us. Know that the summative damage done do you does not add up to an identity, not now, not ever. It does not make you unworthy of healing; it makes you desperately in need of a Savior. There is more to you than the hurt that has been inflicted, *so much more*. Your pain matters, yes, but it is not your entire story. It may define a season, but there is *life* after the bleeding stops, and God intends to use that life to demonstrate His glory. Take note: you were designed with redemption and healing in mind. Jesus suffered a grueling death on a Cross to secure your potential for total restoration, so that others might be drawn to Him through your story—and it is starts with being bold enough to openly share it once you begin the process of healing.

No matter what lies your pain has convinced you of, the underlying goal of enemy's misuse of our pain is to convince us that we are both undeserving and incapable of being healed. He wants us to doubt our own worth and God's ability to fix us at the same time. He wants us to think we are unworthy of loving, and that the wounds we bear somehow render us useless in God's Kingdom. But much like our Savior himself, the scars we carry are actually proof that Satan has tried his hardest to defeat us--and failed miserably. They are the reminders of the battle; yes, evidence of the war, but not badges of defeat.

The truth Satan wants you to forget is this: The tomb is still *empty*. Our Savior did not defeat death on a *superficial* level so that we may be *partially* healed. That is not how the story goes. Jesus eviscerated Satan, stole the keys, and came back in glory because He is a conqueror and as His daughter, so are you...

...but here is the catch. We can hold ourselves back from being fully healed if we do not believe it to be possible. So we must acknowledge the truth of the miracles Jesus has done in order to realign our thinking. Tell me, when in scripture did Jesus leave *anything* halfway accomplished?
Did He leave the lame man with one bum leg?
Did He leave the mute unable to speak?
Did He only halfway correct the blind man's vision?

Certainly not, and He is not in the business of halfway healing us, either.

Despair? Self-hatred? Guilt? Shame? This is not our where our story ends. I can sum our reality for you in exactly two words:

Redemption won.

Redemption won the moment God woke me up in the middle of the night in my college dorm room. Redemption won the moment I fell flat on my face in the presence of the Lord and cried out for help--and was answered. Redemption won the moment Jesus told me that I was *not* too far gone to be saved and I was *not* so dirty that His blood couldn't wash out my stains and I was *not* what the enemy tried to claim as my broken identity. Redemption won the moment Jesus stormed the gates of hell and kicked Satan in the teeth for me. Redemption will win for you, too sister.

While not all of us have suffered under the hands of controlling or toxic relationships, we have all endured seasons of intense and unrelenting pain and grueling loss. Some of it has been inflicted by men and women who hurt us, some of it seemingly an unfair attack on us by the world in its entirety. Regardless of where your hurt comes from, let me encourage you in this truth: You are *more* than the lies that have been crammed into your head. You are *not* damaged goods. You are a *cherished* daughter. You are *fully known* and *fully loved* by the

God who made you. You are *not* too far gone for God's grace, and you never will be. You do not have to be controlled by the pain, nor do you have to handle this on your own. Your stains are *not* permanent. You *can* be completely healed. There is *more* to your story than the worst chapter would have you believe, and God is not finished with you yet.

This harsh truth of pain is this: It changes us. It causes us to alter our thinking and restructures our brains in a manner that does everything its power to avoid feeling *that way* ever again. It is in our nature—to be changed by tragedy. I pray that you find comfort in this: While trauma and hardship do change us, they do not change God. He is the ever-constant, never-failing God who calls Himself the Mighty Counselor. The Abba Father. The Lord Who Sees. The Lord Who Heals. The Lord Who Dwells with Us. He is both Sovereign Lord and Intimate Dad. He is both the God who knows all, and the God who suffers with us in our pain. He is fully present in both our moments of pain and during the journey towards healing.

You can call on the Lord, in the fullness of His presence. Believe that Jehovah Jireh, the Provider, will bring you all that you need to find healing—the right people to walk alongside you, the wisdom to see the truth of how your pain affects you, and the ability to forgive others of inexcusable things just as He has forgiven you of your past mistakes. Know that Jehovah Nissi is your banner. He will fight for your victory, and He's never been in the business of losing. Remember that Jehovah Shalom is a God of peace, wholeness, and order. He is not a God of chaos, and He will not let you drown in yours.

This is the time to acknowledge our pain, dear friend. We all carry it with us. We shove it deep down and try to hide it away, but try as we might, we cannot keep our pain from God with shallow prayers and surface praises. He wants to intercept our pain. He wants to be in the midst of removing it. He wants to create healing where the enemy intended to grow seeds of spiritual death.

Let the Lord into your pain.

I know, I know. This is digging around in some sensitive areas. This is pointing out your scars—maybe some more recently inflicted than others. This is drudging up the old stuff you thought was hidden so well, maybe you would forget it, too.

We must admit, here and now, that sometimes the pain we know feels safer when we hold on to it; to validate our frustrations, to justify our tears and sleepless nights. We are waiting, desperately, for someone to tell us that our pain still *matters*. That we have a *right* to feel the way that we do. The pain we know feels safer than the healing we don't, so we keep our fists wrapped around our hurt and refuse to let anyone in.

Air out the wounds, friend.
It is time to take off the concealer.
Remove the self-made bandages.
Let Him into your pain and hear this:
He doesn't want you to hold on to that any longer.
This is not the way He intended you to live.

This is far easier said than done, I know.

I get that this chapter is not some magical wand you can wave over your wounds, nor is it a time machine that can immediately undo years of damage and hurt inflicted on your heart. I know that some of you literally feel trapped by pain in its many physical, emotional, and spiritual forms. I am not trying to belittle your experience, but rather trying to show you just how *big* our God is, how *powerful* His use of our pain can be for His kingdom, and how *incredible* it feels to experience freedom—even if we must beseech it from Him daily until the infection starts to clear and we can wrap our minds around the fact that healing is *real*.

I say this because once our pain has been fully surrendered to the Lord, there is *nothing, nothing, nothing* in this world that can compare to the victory of redemption. Right now? It hurts. It sucks. It feels unfair. Whatever is going on in your heart in this moment, it is real for you. So let it be *real*. Let it *really* hurt. Call your pain by name and address it head-on, because even if you can not grasp it yet, you are on your way to healing, and God will not forsake you in the repurposing of your pain.

So, where do we go from here? We go to the feet of Jesus—it's the only place of freedom that I know. We grieve our losses, and we grieve them fully. We feel the weight of our wounds and recognize the space in our hearts that has been long inhabited by doubt that we can actually be healed. We say to our pain, "You matter, but you no longer serve a purpose in my life." We open our shaky, white-knuckled hands, and boldly surrender to the pain to our infinitely loving Father.

We cry.
We scream.
We wrestle.
And we are given our new identity.
We are given our freedom.

"Dear ones, do not be surprised when you experience your trial by fire. It is not something strange and unusual, but it is something you should rejoice in. In it you share the Anointed's sufferings, and you will be that much more joyful when His glory is revealed. If anyone condemns you for following *Jesus as* the Anointed One, consider yourself blessed. The glorious Spirit of God rests on you. But none of you should ever merit suffering like those who have murdered or stolen, meddled in the affairs of others or done evil things. But if you should suffer for being a Christian, do not think of it as a disgrace, *as it would be if you had done wrong.* Praise God that you are permitted to carry this name." 1 Peter 4:12-16

Questions for Unlearning

- The pain that you're carrying; where did it come from?

- What have you tried to manage your pain with? Are these habits healthy, and have they been working? Why or why not?

- What would a day without this pain look like for you?

- Do you believe that you can be fully healed from the emotional wounds inflicted upon you? Not for other people; for you. Do you believe this healing is possible for you, in your heart, in your life?

- What's stopping you from letting it go?

- What are some practical steps you can take to acknowledge this pain, its power, and its impact on your heart, so that you can move towards healing?

Challenge Eight

Since this topic is a heavy one, we will approach the accompanying challenge with the gravity the situation deserves. I encourage you to work through the questions for unlearning and spend a few days letting God work in your heart *before you even start* this section. Give yourself some time and space as your thinking is renewed; as you start to view your pain in light of the grand scheme of redemption.

If we seek to change the ways we view our pain within our Christian circles, we have to do the hard and worthy work of opening up to the believers in our proximity. We have to to let them know how we've been hurt, and the incredible reality of restoration accomplished for us by Christ. In order to do this, I challenge you to share the raw, unfiltered version of your story with someone this week. Be it a close friend over coffee, at your small group on Monday night, or with someone unexpected the Lord puts on your heart, I encourage you to boldly share the truth of your story. There is such power in our vulnerability, and great potential for our communities when we give others the space to say, "Me, too."

A few notes I humbly ask that you will consider regarding this challenge:

- Pray, pray, pray. For the person you will be sharing with, for your ability to open up, and for God's power to be revealed in your story.

- Give your person, whoever you are sharing with, a heads up! It may make for an awkward conversation if they aren't given some context for the conversation you are hoping to have.

- Work through what you want to say *before* you meet with them. When our raging emotions take over, it can be easy to get sidetracked, for pain to sneak back in and attempt to take over the story. Making a few notes ahead of time can help you stay focused on one, the truth of what your pain has looked like, and two, the reality of redemption that has overcome it.

- Allow the person you're sharing with time to digest and respond. They may reciprocate by sharing some hard things, too.

- Don't share if you are not ready. If the pain you are dealing with is extremely recent, highly traumatic, or may trigger feelings of panic by revisiting it, I caution you to only share if you feel safe enough to do so. This may need to look more like a counselor's chair or a pastor's office than a coffee shop with your BFF, and *that is okay.* If you feel that you would best benefit from sharing about your pain with someone emotionally and spiritually equipped to handle it with the wisdom and sensitivity it demands, please do so on your own time as you feel able.

Let Us Pray

Father God, we come before you, silent. Not to ask for anything. Not to accuse you. Not to get anything in return. We come to you, to leave it all at your feet. We come before you with empty hands and open hearts because Lord, we need you. We cannot heal without you. We cannot make sense of our pain without you. We cannot move from this place until we've surrendered our hurt and surrendered it fully. So, today, we come to you on our knees. We come in our brokenness. In our fear. In our hurt. In our confusion. We come to heal in your presence. We come to be filled. We come to be made whole. We come to sit before your throne, and wait for you to move.

Anxiety & Cold Coffee

My anxiety is a cold cup of coffee.

It feels like I am trapped in a tiny, sail-less boat, being tossed around by a monsoon of emotions.
I want to have a say in what parts of my life anxiety can and cannot touch.
I want to learn how to manage my anxiety on my terms—not to be controlled by its endless demands.
I want to let dishes sit in the sink and laundry in the hamper, and not pace around the house all day trying to clean every little thing I see that is imperfect.

Yes, my anxiety is a cold cup of coffee that has been forgotten in the microwave for the tenth time today. Usually, by the time I have my coffee in the morning, it has already started. As I pace around in circles, I see everything that is out of place. I see everything that needs to be done for the day. Most people will make a mental note. Some may even write a list down on paper. Me? Oh, it is nothing serious (I tell myself as I fight off another urge to look up anxiety medications yet again). I do not write lists. I do not make mental notes. I clean it then and there.

I walk around from mess to mess, armed with nervous energy and adrenaline and anxiety, because my brain tells me that it is not right until it is clean, until it is perfect. So there sits my coffee. Abandoned in the microwave because what starts off as a trip to the bathroom ends in a two-hour cleaning frenzy that cannot wait until later. Truthfully? I cannot even remember the last time I sat down and stayed put long enough to drink an entire mug of hot coffee.

This, my friends, is why I consider my anxiety a problem.
This is why I want to unlearn the habits it has created in my
mind and heart.

Maybe you'd like to unlearn yours, too?

Much like a pen stain on my favorite dress, I am worried that if
someone looks hard and long enough, they will *see* my anxiety. I
am worried it will never go away, that it cannot be washed out. I
am worried, period. That is the nature of the thing at its core. It
is the gnawing feeling in the pit of my stomach that keeps me
from unwinding and relaxing and otherwise resting. It tells me
that I can't, I shouldn't, and I flat out don't deserve to take it
easy.

This may be part the biggest problem we face when we deal
with anxiety—you cannot simply close that tab on your browser
when you are done with it for the day. It is a consuming thing
that tries to bleed over into every area of your life like a red
sock in a load of whites.

One of the important first steps for us, as society and as
believers in particular, is to unlearn what we feel and think
towards mental illness. As the whole collective body of Jesus-
loving humans, we have seriously got it wrong. It both confuses
and angers me that we have advanced so far in incredible ways,
but we still seem to be stuck in the mud when it comes to
perceptions of emotional disorders. It burdens me to know that
so many of us sit in our churches on Sunday morning afraid to
be honest, afraid to admit the darkness of our struggles, and
afraid to be judged by the Christ followers around us.

I am not sure how your anxiety manifests itself in your life, if
you struggle with it in any capacity. Statistics tell me that it is
likely the majority of you reading this book have dealt with
some form of emotional disorder or mental illness in your

lifetime, or deal with it still.

Depression. Anxiety. OCD. PTSD. ODD. BDD. I have worked with girls, namely trauma victims, with these disorders enough to recognize the cycles of thinking and therefore behavior that accompanies them. But I am not a therapist and more importantly, I am not *your* therapist. You have every right to read what I have to say in this chapter and tell me to stick it where the sun don't shine, though the people pleasing anxiety in me is hoping that you won't.

So, rather than address the specific nature of something you may or may not struggle with, I want us to first focus our attention on some cold, hard truth regarding mental illness. What it is. What it is not. What the bible has to say on the matter. How we can learn to hold on to hope. This way, even though you may not deal with this issue yourself, you can be an advocate and peacemaker for someone in your life who does. Trust me, it is worth your time. I wish with all my heart more people were informed about the implications that mental illness has on us as believers.

The lies our religious bubbles tell us about mental illness are also many in number, and have undoubtedly added to their detrimental affects on how we view ourselves in the wake of the struggle. So let us clear up one of the common myths about mental illness and be done with it for good. Your depression? Anxiety? OCD? Other combination of letters that a therapist slapped on you to label your behavior? It does not define you. Hold that diagnosis, whatever it is, in your hand for a moment and stare it down. Look it in the eyes and tell it, *"you do not define me."*

All that label means, friend, is that it is the closest thing that resembled your behaviors and thought life the day you walked into your therapist's office. It is simply a word that everyone agreed to use in a situation that looks like yours. It is limited to being a fancy term for the imbalance of neurochemicals in your head that create a corresponding obsession and compulsion. It is used to describe a hormone level that affects your mood significantly. It is many things, yes, but it is not your identity.

I will come clean with you here. I used to genuinely believe the lie that "real Christians" could not be depressed. They could not have anxiety, OCD, or any other combination of letters emanating from a psychiatrist's office. I believed, at the urging of the church, that depression and anxiety were not real for Christ followers—maybe you did, too. I was raised by a society and in such a time that if you were sad, you just prayed and it was supposed to magically go away. If you had any difficult thing in your life, including depression, you swept it under the rug, pretended it never happened, and told everyone on Sunday morning that you were highly favored by the Good Lord. *Too blessed to be stressed*, anyone?

You can imagine my shock and confusion when I got through the majority of a psychology degree and had learned of things like chemical imbalances, hereditary dispositions, and misfiring neurotransmitters that all contribute to various degrees and presentations of mental illness. You can imagine my reluctance to admit that I myself have likely suffered from an anxiety disorder for most of my adult life, if not longer. Yeah. That pill was hard to swallow and it tasted pretty awful going down.

The truth is that mental illness is not evidence of spiritual weakness. Righteousness does not always equate with sanity, ya dig? Even the most "renowned believers" you can think of can struggle with mental illness because it is just that, an illness. Depression does not exist because you have not prayed hard enough. Anxiety does not take over because you are actively rejecting peace. You do not suffer because you have not logged enough hours in your prayer closet. As ridiculous as it sounds on paper, I know the ways these lies can work into our beliefs about ourselves. They cause guilt, feelings of shame, and the belief that we are being punished. This is not so, friend.

For those of us who have considered, tried, or tried to no avail to pursue a medical relief to the static of anxiety or weight of depression, there can be much secrecy surrounding our efforts to find healing. We feel as though we must hide our attempts to make progress, whether that be in the counselor's office, the pharmacy refilling our Xanax, or the daily affirmations we make holding onto the truth of who we really are. To the thoughts, and people, who have told you that medication is the devil, or that "good Christians" should not take mood-stabilizing medication, we say good riddance. There is an element of wisdom in seeking help, an attitude of humility in admitting that we cannot do this alone.

Look at it this way: If I tripped walking up the stairs and sprained my ankle, what would you advise me to do? Would you tell me to suck it up, walk it off, and get over it? Would you tell me that the pain is all in my head, and I am probably making it up? Would you steal my crutches and claim that it is an elaborate rouse to get attention? Would you tell me that it only hurts because I do not believe strongly enough that God will heal my ankle? Hell no.

You would tell me to go see a doctor, expect me to obtain a diagnosis, and if it is bad enough, to see a physical therapist to aid in its healing. It sounds ridiculous when we talk like that about a physical injury, doesn't it? So why is it the norm when we speak of mental or emotional illness in that light?

Thanks to God's grace and my own season of unlearning, I now see these mental illnesses for what they really are: proof that we are in a broken world where things are out of order, and we do not always have the luxury of knowing why. My desire is that others would come to realize that any emotional or mental or psychological issue someone has is just that—an issue. It is an illness in need of treatment and circumstance we are living in. It is not a choice, nor is it a fad. It is not an excuse to take medication. It is not the easy way out of anything. If you struggle in this at any level, you know fully well there is nothing easy about it. There is nothing weak-minded about it. There is no sin that caused it and it is not a part of our lives for a lack of prayer. It is a circumstance of living in a fallen world and it flat out *sucks*. No one chooses to live this way. My hope is that we will learn to focus less about the why of mental illness, and more about where to go from here.

This is one of the bigger obstacles we face walking through this maze: recognizing truthful conviction from the Holy Spirit from the lies anxiety and depression tell us in an attempt to derail our progress. That is how the enemy works, and this is how he uses our minds against us. You see, his voice focuses on the apparent flaws in our own character, while the Holy Spirit reminds us of God's unwavering, faithful, redemptive character.

To bring it back to our thought life, we have the difficult and necessary task before us of discerning the good thoughts from the bad. To figure out which ones are honest enough to spur us towards progress, and which ones are lies of the enemy meant to keep us circling around the same flawed messages. This can be increasingly difficult when compounded with the mess of anxiety, the numbing haze of depression, or any other challenge that hinders our ability to think clearly. Even so, we must learn to hold each thought in our hands and determine its origin. Once we can understand how to separate the lies from truth; we will be on our way to managing not only our anxiety and depression, but a whole host of identity issues that contribute to it.

As we move forward, I encourage you to remember these truths: Anxiety had a first day, and it will have a last. It is a circumstance, not a sin. Do you hear that? Anxiety is not a sin. Depression is not a sin. Fatigue and exhaustion and feeling stuck in a rut? Those are not sins, either.

What they are is evidence of a broken world. They are reminders that this earth is not our home and we are surely, increasingly far from the Garden where all things were in order. They demonstrate our infinite need for a Savior. They create in us a craving for peace and to trust the authority of Christ that we otherwise may not understand. They can be used to draw us into a place of beautiful and radical dependence on God, if we let Him use these chaotic moments for His glory.

Every breath, even the ones that are hard to take, belong to Him.
Every heartbeat, even the ones choked by panic, are proof that there is still life in our veins and purpose to our days.

Anxiety is the habit of fear, and today, we take the first hesitant and widely over-analyzed step towards kicking it to the curb. Who's with me?

We can say this boldly now, but we all know be it a few hours or days from now, that we will likely backslide into the pit that our illness has dug for us. You may fall back into the patterns of your depression and chaos-as-normal way of functioning. And you know what? That is okay. I am here to tell you; it is going to be okay.

Our progress may not look like progress to anyone else—but we don't have to let that discourage us from appreciating the breakthroughs, big or small. Progress is different things to different people, and no one else gets to define it but the one that's doing the work. For some of us, a breakthrough is getting up and sticking to our schedule for a day or a week or a month if you are feeling ambitious. For some of us, it may be grocery shopping and sticking to a budget. For others, it looks like getting through your workday without a panic attack. Whereas one person's progress is letting dirty dishes sit in the sink, another's may be not letting them sit there for too long.

It is all progress, it all *counts*. Let that sink in. Every step you take towards health and healing? It counts, no matter how tiny it seems. It does not matter if you take two steps back half an hour later. In that moment, on that day, you stuck it to your (insert struggle) and *that* is significant. Do not let anyone else take that victory away because it deserves to be celebrated and your achievement deserves to be noticed.

This is how we unlearn. We face this head on, and that can be a difficult thing to do. Thankfully the Bible is chocked full of wisdom for those of us drowning in the chaos. I told you at the start of the chapter that I feel like a tiny sail-less boat being tossed around by my anxiety. What scripture tells me is that Jesus is both the anchor that grounds me and the lighthouse that guides me back to sanity. Please do not misunderstand this, I am not suggesting that your struggles are the result of failing to pray hard enough or read the right scriptures or ask God pretty, pretty please with a cherry on top. I know, and you know, that is not how this works.

What I *am* suggesting is that Jesus is here to bring glimmers of hope. Moments of peace. Days of lessened burdens. Weeks of joy. Much of life is not composed of the mountaintop moments. Our struggles with anxiety and depression are not any different. It is the small, patched together steps towards progress that compose the story of our victory. It is little battle after little battle that advance us towards health and healing. Which, by the way, is always the goal, right?

For me, this season of learning how to manage my anxiety has been expectedly difficult; yes, but not in the way I anticipated. I have had to unlearn the lies I grew up hearing in church. I have had to figure out how to stop blaming myself for the bad days, and the really bad days. I have had to learn how to show grace to myself in the moments I need to step out of a seemingly normal situation because I have that knot in the pit of my stomach that precedes a panic attack. I have had to learn how to say no to things that will cause me unhealthy stress. I have had to draw hard boundaries that exclude people in my life that are at the end of the day, toxic. I have had to undo years, and years, of guilt that have been piled onto my identity. I have had to admit the harsh but necessary reality; anxiety and depression are not battles of will. I cannot defeat it by fighting harder and doing more. I can only find peace when I sit at the feet of Jesus, doing and striving and fighting less. It all seems so backwards. It is hard work. It is work. Period. It takes guts, stamina, and an ability to look inward while not forgetting to dwell on things above. It is complicated and messy and feels like untangling twenty-year-old Christmas lights from grandma's attic, so we must all be patient with ourselves in the process.

As for all of those people who have asked you if you have tried yoga, suggested you try their magical herbal tea that's sure to "cure your depression", invited you to a prayer meeting so they can "cast out your disabling spirit", told you that mood stabilizing medication is the devil, blinked twice and claimed that real Christians simply cannot have a mental illness, and related your OCD to the way they like their pillows just so on their sofa,

let it go.

Do not be angry towards their ignorance. Do not spend your good time and energy dwelling on the ideas they are spouting at you. Take a deep breath, recognize their lack of knowledge and authority on your life and your emotions, and let it go if you are able.

Truthfully, I still do not have all of the specific answers we each need for unlearning the anxiety or depression or burden that we are sitting under. What I do know is that there are scriptures and pieces of Jesus' character that I hold onto with everything I have on the days when it all seems to fall to apart. I know that Jesus has not abandoned us to struggle in this alone. I know that I have had anxiety-free moments that serve as tiny glimpses of heaven, reminding me that this world is not ultimately my home.

I have led you through the wilderness for 40 years. The clothes on your back and the sandals on your feet haven't worn out. You haven't had bread to eat or wine or strong drink to consume, but I've fed you each day with manna so you'd know that I, the Eternal, am your God who protects you and provides for you." Deuteronomy 29:5-6

Sometimes I feel like anxiety, depression, and complete hopelessness must have been a part of the Israelites suffering through forty years of walking in the wilderness. While it may be easy for us to shake our heads in disbelief at their lack of faith, we must see this story, too, with fresh eyes. It is easy for us to shout, "Don't you see that God is leading you to the Promised Land?" when we can read the story from the comfort of our couches.

It is an entirely different picture when we immerse ourselves into this scene. As we wander through our own deserts, how many times have we doubted the Lord's faithfulness? How many times have we looked up to heaven, with an open mouth and a closed heart and shouted, "Lord. When will I get out of this wilderness? Where are you leading me? Shouldn't I be there by now?"

Take heart, because God sees our whole story, and it is far from over.

So in whatever wilderness it feels like you are walking through, remember this: *our sandals are not worn out just yet.* We are still being fed. God has us right where He wants us, and we are going to make it out of this desert. God has not left us stranded in the wilderness without sustenance, without hope, or without a final destination. We simply have not reached our promised land *yet...*

...and I cannot reasonably guarantee you that we will reach it on this side of eternity. That may sound negative or discouraging, but my prayer is that we find comfort as we shift our thinking into remembering this truth: We are not really supposed to be all that comfortable in this world to begin with. We must remember, this is not our eternal home. We have not yet made it back to our Shalom, but we are getting closer by the day.

Maybe we are souls of a different kind, you and I. Maybe our spirits are rightly sensitive to the tension of living in this broken world that is desperately awaiting the return of its Savior. Maybe our anxiety and depression and the days we cannot pull ourselves out of the mess are the days that teach us to dwell on eternity in ways we would never otherwise understand. Maybe our hearts are not at rest because they long for the garden in ways our human minds cannot digest.

This, I can assure you.
There will be no anxiety in heaven.
There will be no depression when we see Jesus face to face.
There will be no addiction, no need for medication, no panic attacks, and no guilt for our mental status when we kneel before the throne.
There will be only praise.
There will be only peace.
There will be a fullness of healing when we are restored and presented as saints without blemish, and we will be made whole.

Until that holy moment comes, we must hold on to hope. We must let Jesus fight with us in this battle and admit that we cannot do it alone. Haven't we tried that? It certainly did not work out so well for me, I can only assume it did not do you much good, either.

So to the lies, we learn and believe a new response.
When Satan confronts you with, "If God was really for you and

not against you, wouldn't He have healed you by now?" We can respond with, "My God can heal me, and I will choose to trust Him even if He does not do so until I reach the other side of eternity. He will work all things, even your attacks and lies, together for my good and His glory." When challenged with, "God will heal you, you just need to pray harder and have more faith." We can say, "God has not healed me yet because He longs for me to increasingly depend on Him. It is up to me to trust that He *can* even if He chooses *not to do so yet.*" When attacked with the lie that says, "This is as good at it gets," we refute it with the Word of God in Romans that says,

"Now I'm sure of this: the sufferings we endure now are not even worth comparing to the glory that is coming and will be revealed in us." Romans 8:18

As we start this process, our anxiety or depression may tell us that being still is a failure. It is crucial to remember God's truth that tells us to be still is actually the *first step* to claiming victory. We can find comfort in knowing that Jesus Himself rested while He was on earth. How foolish of us, in our flesh, to assume we can survive any other way. Only when we learn to truly rest in His presence will we start to see progress.

This is the truth: not only is God going to fight our battle, He is going to win it. Fact check? Satan loses in the end. Anxiety loses in the end. Depression loses in the end--and it is not solely up to us to make sure that happens. So if the victory has not been won for you yet, it is not because you lose the war, it is because your story is not yet over. Our responsibility in this is to know the God that wins the war more fully, to trust Him more completely, and to allow Him to teach us that progress will look exactly how He wants it to.

"The Eternal One has responded to your pleading, 'Do not fear or worry about this army. This battle is not yours to fight; it is the True God's. Tomorrow, they will travel through the ascent of Ziz. Meet them at the end of the valley before the

wilderness of Jerul. There, I will be watching. Stand and watch, but do not fight the battle. There, you will watch the Eternal save you, Judah, and Jerusalem. Do not fear or worry. Tomorrow, face the army and trust that Eternal is with you."
2nd Chronicles 20:15-17

"There is a sure way for us to know that we belong to the truth. Even though our inner thoughts may condemn us *with storms of guilt and constant reminders of our failures,* we can know in our hearts that in His presence God Himself is greater than any accusation. He knows all things."
1st John 3:19-20

"He's above all rule, authority, power, and dominion; over every name invoked, *over every title bestowed* in this age and the next." Ephesians 1:21

Questions for Unlearning

- In what ways have issues such as anxiety, depression, or worry impacted my life?

- What habits have I formed, good or bad, to manage these issues?

- What lies do my anxiety, depression, or worry tell me about myself?

- What parts of Jesus and His character can I hold on to when I need to combat these lies?

- What are some practical, small victories I can look forward to celebrating as I move towards health and healing?

- What are the truths about my situation that I've been avoiding, and how can I come to terms with them?

- What parts of this do I hold back from God?

- What would a day without anxiety or worry look like?

Challenge Nine

For those of you who struggle

This challenge is short, but I want your *full* attention for it. We can do a good and hard thing here by saying this truth out loud (I will if you will). Fill the blanks in below with whatever anxiety, stress, depression, or current struggle you are living in. Keep this truth written down somewhere that you will see it daily. Whether that's on your phone, by the coffee pot, or in the front of your Bible, be sure to read over it when you are feeling discouraged or overwhelmed.

Breathe and repeat,

"My _____ is not a sin. This _____ is not God punishing me for a mistake that I have made in the past. This _____ is not payback for something I have done that I regret. This _____ does not take away my salvation. This _____ does not lessen the potency and totality of my redemption. This _____ does not make the work that Jesus did on the Cross for me any less significant and victorious and this _____ does not alter the foundation on which my hope is built."

Next, I want you to keep track of any small or big steps you take this week towards progress, and celebrate them! Even the smallest victory is worthy of recognition. Whether it's sticking to your schedule, finishing everything on your to-do list, or showing grace to yourself during the bad days, be sure to give thanks for the ability to make and see progress, and allow yourself space to be proud of the accomplishment. Keep the notes handy so that on the days when life seems overwhelming in its entirety, you can remember the times you kicked your anxiety or depression in the face, and thank the God who invites us to work towards healing.

For those of you who don't

Chances are, someone in your life has struggled or currently struggles with some form of mental illness. My challenge to you in this is to increase your understanding of what they struggle with, particularly, and make an effort to reach out to them. Offer to pray with them, ask how their treatment is going, or simply be a shoulder to cry on if that's what they need. By acting as an informed advocate for them, you can be a part of removing the stigma of mental illness in our Christian communities. Secondly, I will ask you to keep your eyes and mind open to conversations about mental illness as you encounter them. Look for opportunities to speak truth about issues like anxiety and depression, as we seek to change the picture regarding our treatment of believers who suffer under these types of burdens.

Let Us Pray

Lord, we come to you with our clouded thinking and our weary hearts. We admit to you that sometimes anxiety and depression are overwhelming realities for us, or for those we hold dear. We surrender to you the lies that tell us mental illness is an indicator of sin, and ask that you remove any false sense of guilt we carry for the times panic and doubt. We submit to your truth that says our shalom and fullness of healing are coming, and we accept that this may not be until we reach heaven. We trust that you desire to grow our faith through the days where life feels overwhelming, and we ask that you give us the wisdom to seek help, guidance, and accountability as we progress towards total health. We admit that our ideas about healing and progress look busy and efforts-based, just like the world around us. Change this picture in our minds, Lord. We ask that you reveal to us the beauty of sitting still at your feet, and that we would learn to truly rest in your presence as our first line of defense against our sometimes misleading emotions. We are dependent on you to change our hearts, steady our minds, and brings us moments of victory that inspire us to hope against hope that you are at work in us, even in the midst of the chaos.

The Power of Fear

Maybe we all need to be reminded that God really is bigger than the boogeyman, anxiety, and other scary things.

After talking to countless women, I examined their responses to a simple yet powerful question. When asked, "What is your biggest fear?" I found some revealing and haunting truth.

Women expressed, almost unanimously, that their fear is a *constant* struggle. These were not scenario-specific fears limited to public speaking or heights or flying on airplanes. These fears were deeply rooted, firmly established patterns they based their life around. The fear of losing a husband or child. The fear of being abandoned. The fear of being a disappointment. The fear of being forgotten, ending up alone, dying before living a full life, the inability to have children, and the fear of missing opportunity.

These are not lightly weighted fears. These are *heavy* chains we are carrying, sister, and you are not alone in this terrifying struggle. It took very little prompting or time for these women to open up to me. They did not need hours to think or discern what they feared most. These fears were deeply rooted, yes, but also very near to the surface as it remained present on their minds. Fear may feel like an irremovable part of our being, but this is not how we were intended to live. This rock is not a worthy, fruit-bearing burden that we are carrying.

We are told in scripture that we are given a sound mind—so where is the disconnect? How do we get from being kept in perfect peace to building our lives around avoiding the things

we fear most? How do we get from securely in the grasp of
Jesus to installing emotional safety nets just in case something
goes wrong? If we were not given a spirit of fear—where do the
nightmares come from?

Here is some widely-overlooked truth for us to dive into: even
those Jesus hand-picked, trained, and invested the most in
during His time walking the earth seem to have their own trust
issues when they face things that scare them.

For example, remember the story with the wind and waves?
You know the one in Mark 4, where the disciples all have panic
attacks as the boat is being tossed around by the powerful
storm? There are some important implications here when we
dig a little deeper. Let us set the scene.

Jesus has had a seriously long day. After the crowds have been
dismissed, and everyone goes home, it is time for Jesus and His
followers to go to the other side of the sea of Galilee. All seems
right with the world...until they get in the boat.

It starts to pour, lightning strikes, and the waves quickly turn
violent. We are not talking about a little spring rainfall, here.
This is a full-on, hurricane season, hunker-down type of storm.
While the disciples are, well, panicking, Jesus is sleeping on a
sandbag under the boat.

Wait, what?

Yes, that's right. Jesus sleeps until His disciples wake Him.
There are three vastly important things we need to recognize in
this story, and they have nothing to do with the part where
Jesus actually calms the storm.

For one thing, Jesus was silent as He slept below His panicked
followers, but He was not out of control. How often do we
mistake Jesus' silence for inactivity and inability to step in and

rescue us? We assume that because He is not engaged that He must be unaware of the storm. Honestly, how many times have we read this verse and scratched our heads as our Savior sleeps while His followers are almost drowning, literally, in the chaos?

The second thing we see is this: the disciples jump to the worst case scenario. Sound familiar, anyone? When they wake Jesus, their words to Him are, *"Master! Don't you care we are about to die?"* In other words, they did not wake Him seeking a Savior—they woke Him seeking answers as to why they had not yet been saved. They both assumed the worst and questioned His love, all in a single breath. Their response to Jesus echoes our human nature and its reaction to panic. Fear makes us question the Lord's intentions, and doubt that He is still good. It frames our mind to think, "He cannot save me, nor does He want to." This is why we desperately plea for a life raft, instead of believing He will calm the storm. So we ask for far too little, because we do not trust His character.

Thirdly, we see the followers of Jesus in true form during this hurricane. By the time they wake Jesus, they are convinced the story is already over. Have you ever looked at them with critical eyes and wondered how they could doubt; how could they be afraid? Jesus is physically present with them, and yet they remain paralyzed by fear.

Don't they know that Jesus has this covered?
Don't they know He's about to calm the storm?

I encourage you, to look honestly at the way we handle our fear. We, too, feel as though we might drown in the chaos. We doubt our Savior. We, like the disciples, are paralyzed by fear and panic with Jesus standing right next to us in our boats. If someone were to see our whole story, I imagine they would respond the same way I have reacted to the disciples for years when reading this passage.

"Hey, guys, don't you know He's about to rescue you?"

Luckily for us, the disciples' response to fear lets us know that humankind is no stranger to feelings of panic, despair, and doubt. We panic when the situation seems too far beyond our control. We despair when we feel helpless to change the outcome. We doubt that God is big enough to handle it, because we forget that He is with us in the boat.

Though the disciples get a bad rap for this scene, I think the most important part of all is Jesus' response—and not the one where He says, "Peace, Be Still". We tend to skim past this because we know the story by heart, and in doing so, we miss the significance of Jesus's heart towards His fearful followers. Maybe we have missed His heart towards fear entirely.

When all is said and done, after Jesus calms the storm, He asks an important question. You'll notice He does not ask, "What are you so afraid of?" No, He does not question them about the things they fear most or ask what they thought would happen if He failed to calm the storm. Jesus' question here is fundamentally different and should absolutely change our thought life about fear.

He asks the disciples, *"Why are you so afraid?"*

Let this question sit with you for a moment, and hear this: Jesus does not ask us *what* we are afraid of; He asks us *why* we fear. He does not ask us what we think the outcome will be. He doe not ask us for our backup plan. He does not ask us to list out the things that grip us with fear and panic and despair, because He *already* knows. Will you grasp that with me? He already knows what you are afraid of. That has never been the question.

You see, if Jesus asked us what we were afraid of, it would serve to prove His power over those scary things. However, Jesus does not phrase it quite that way. Since He asks us why we are afraid, this turns the question not to "Is He powerful enough to destroy the things we are afraid of?", but, "Are we willing to trust that He will?"

The question of fear has never been about God's power—it has eternally been a question of our trust in Him to do the things we cannot, to step out in faith when fear has our feet stuck in cement, to believe that He is who He says He is. We must unlearn this habit of fear, and replace it with trust. Take a deep breath, this is going to be hard because these habits run deep.

We learn fear from a young age; what it is, when to feel it, what to do with it. As children we are taught to recognize situations that warrant fear and respond to them with urgency. Think back to learning about "stranger danger", when you were taught to avoid people that you did not know because they could be dangerous.

Remember back to early teachings about Jesus. Maybe you were taught to be afraid of hell and eternal separation from Him. In fact, we often hear about salvation in terms of fear. It is used to scare people into salvation who are seeking an escape route from hell and death and damnation. Let us understand: This is not the heart of Jesus. It is about so much more than fear and scare tactics. That is not how the future of our hearts needs to be addressed. The Gospel is not the easy way out—it is the only way out. Salvation is *not* the product of fear—it is the only answer to it. We do not choose Jesus because we are afraid. He has already chosen us and is simply waiting for the response to His invitation to a life that operates outside of fear's jurisdiction.

Hopefully it is clear to you that fear is a deeply rooted construct in our flesh. We feel it deeply. We avoid the things that provoke it constantly. We have likely made an idol, at one time or another, out of appeasing our own fears. When we dig a little deeper, we find that fear comes from two places in our hearts.

The first reason we often turn to fear is because we doubt. Either we doubt that we are capable of confronting a fear, or farther down the rabbit hole, we fear that our God is unable to handle it. I believe fear is its own form of addiction. The more we do it, the easier it is to do. There is a complicated process in the brain that allows this to happen, so I will sum it up in this way: the neurological pathways in our brain that lead to fear and pain are more easily activated the more that they are used. In a nutshell: The more we fear; the more easily we feel afraid. It creates a vicious, haunting cycle. Maybe you are feeling trapped by it, but we are not left alone in the storm to find our own life raft. We must reclaim the certainty in God's character if we want to refute the doubt that plagues our hearts.

The second reason we fear is a misappropriation of power. While I may fear driving in the rain, because I am convinced a terrible and fatal car crash is imminent at every drizzle, the truth of that fear is this: I have attributed all of the power to the rain, and none of the power to myself, the driver, the roads, where I am, the safety of the car, the protection in place, or the Lord Himself. This is precisely what fear does: it puts the assumed power of a situation into the hands of something that we cannot control. This is how fear works, and why it is so effective.

Hold on to hope, though, because the moment we fully realize that even the greatest things we fear—like death or loss of a loved one or failure—have already been overcome and reside next to us in the hands of our Creator, these things we fear start to lose that power.

Feelings of overwhelming anxiety often claim their stake using fear as the primary weapon. Beyond daily stress or a response to a tumultuous life stage, anxiety is fear's playground—and it's got muddy shoes that like to make a big mess of things. It plays on our seemingly rational fears at first. Typically based on a previous experience, it is something that seems just *within* the reach of a plausible scenario. It always starts with a fear that *almost* makes sense, and then it grows inside of us like weeds in a garden. It steals all of our sustenance and withers our once-healthy growth. It keeps the reign of peace from reaching our roots. Most notably—it can take away our ability to bear fruit if we let it.

We must realize that fear only has power over us when we choose to concede to it. This power is great, and can steal the joy from our lives. This is where fear works its way into our relationships, our discipleship, and our honesty with others about where we stand in our emotional state. If there's one single lie that fear loves to tell, it's that no one will care enough about your fears to help you move beyond them. It keeps us from telling others that we are afraid. It keeps us looking inward to appease the fear, instead of looking up to see that Jesus will overcome it.

Fear also paralyzes us, steals our breath, and keeps us unable to breathe deeply and move freely. It is a ball and chain that we carry around each day, only instead of our bodies getting stronger, the ball keeps getting heavier—until we are immobilized by it completely. This is the goal of fear: it wants us to stay exactly where we are, thinking exactly the way that we do.

Fear blurs our vision and makes us see monsters in the midst of shadows. I love using the analogy of fear being like driving in the rain. Maybe this is because driving in a thunderstorm triggers my panic and anxiety in such a huge way, I can explain it to you vividly and honestly. One of the reasons I hate driving in the rain with such passion is because I *hate* not being able to see. Isn't that the truth of fear, though? The things we attribute the power to are often the things that steal our vision. This can be literal, like for me and a torrential downpour in my Nissan. This can also be, and largely is, an issue of spiritual vision in our lives. Fear wants to keep us from seeing the big picture. Maybe it has even convinced you that there is no bigger picture. That is a lie, friend.

You might be stuck in a single point on a map, maybe it feels like the edge of a cliff. All you see is the height of the ledge. All you can think about is how many rocks are at the bottom or how far the fall will be or how long it will be before help can get to you. What you cannot see is the final destination; the overlook of the mountain you've climbed. So many times, friends, we miss the beauty of the hike because we are viewing the journey with the lens of fear.

I cannot speak for you, but I have certainly spent enough of my life letting fear sit in the driver's seat. It has taken me to dark, desperate places. From a young age, even as young as six years old, panic and fear have played major roles in my life. It keeps me cooped up my apartment on days when I fear the world around me in its overwhelming entirety. It keeps me from being honest and transparent on the pages of this book. It keeps me from many things, but I am declaring and believing that the reign of fear in my life is at its end. I am choosing to hold onto peace in the midst of uncertainty instead of fear in the realm of the known.

I know the things I fear most, I imagine you know yours, too. I know them well, as they know me. They laugh at me. They tell us we are not good enough. They tell us we are alone. They tell us no one will listen. They tell us the most extravagant of lies and deep, deep down at our core, we have believed them.

I have let fear run rampant with locks and chains on the dreams that God Himself has given me. I have a gut feeling that you have, too. So let this be the place where we draw a line in the sand and say, *no more*. Let this be the season that we discover God's heart for removing the fear. Let this be the time and place where fear becomes nothing more than a shadow in the night— it only has power in the darkness, and Jesus Christ has come to be our Light. Maybe these monsters we see lurking around every corner are just shadows, dear friend—nothing more than illusions meant to keep us quiet when we have such beautiful stories to tell, to keep us still when such mighty work is yet to be done through us.

The Lord is faithful and is still working in me, but I wonder how much I have already missed because of fear. You could even say I am afraid to realize the things fear has stolen from me. It runs deep. We spend most of our lives learning what we should be afraid of, but this is not the way we were created to live. This is not the life we were made for.

So how do we unlearn our fears, if they are so deeply embedded into our beings? This is a biggie. This is no walk in the park. This is an all-out war on the darkness that tries to steal our courage by using fear as its primary weapon. This is walking into enemy territory with a target on our backs—threatening the mission. Claiming that victory belongs to those whose hope is in the Lord. Destroying the altars we have built to appeasing our fears and comfort and hiding away from doing the hard things because, well, they are hard. This is a big step, and not one we should take haphazardly. We must walk intentionally in this valley, as it is full of land mines and potholes and distractions. But if we press on, as we press on, we get closer and closer to the heart of Jesus who says that He casts out all fear.

This is the ultimate challenge. Are you up for it?

We first need to recognize our fears and call 'em like we see 'em. We need to take a good, hard emotional inventory to take stock of the things we fear most. Let us not lose our momentum by dwelling on the darkness, but rather keep our gaze upward to the Savior that defeated death. We must keep our minds on the moment Jesus stormed the gates of hell. Remember that we fight this battle in full knowledge and faith that Jesus has already won the war.

The Bible invests a lot of space to discussing fear. This is our first clue-in that this fear junk means serious business. However, this should also prove to bring us some comfort here. Take heart in knowing that all men and women who have walked the earth before us have encountered fear. Fear is a common denominator of humankind—we have all felt it deep in our core, and have altered the way we live to appease it. But today, we change that narrative. Today, we shout into the darkness that our God is bigger. Today, we declare victory and life and light and redemption over the parts of ourselves locked up in chains of fear. Today, we press on towards the goal of knowing Jesus more fully, and trusting Him more completely.

So, how do we prevent fear from becoming an idol? And how do we dethrone the things we fear most in the process? The anti-venom to the sting of fear is trust. We must place our fears in the hands of the Almighty, and release them fully. Trust puts the burden from our weary shoulders into the hands of an infinitely powerful God. Trust brings Jesus into our moments of fear and panic and weakness so that we do not suffer alone. Trust takes away the paralyzing notion that our success depends solely upon ourselves.

So, where do we go from here? As you finish this chapter, I want you to hear this straight from my heart. Fear does not disqualify us from greatness. Fear does not make God any less powerful. Fear is a master manipulator that has played our hearts like a fiddle since the day we entered the world, but it does not have the final say. Jesus Christ had the final say, and guess what? He says it is finished. The deficits caused by fear have been paid in full. The work of victory over panic is completely done. The moment he stormed the gates of hell and kicked Satan in the pants, fear lost its power over us. Since Jesus has already defeated death—every lesser thing, depression and anxiety and the boogeyman, are under His authority. Fear cannot hold a candle to the moment Jesus stole the keys of hell and killed death. Remember that as you reflect on the fear in your life. Remember that as you pray.

Now, we must boldly go forward. We must go in confidence. We can go in peace. We go in faith. We go knowing that the Lord himself has already gone before us and accomplished the unthinkable on our behalf. We beat the hell out of fear and start living a life out of the abundant grace given to us moment by moment.

Questions for Unlearning

- What are my biggest fears?

- What do I believe about them?

- How have I rearranged my life to appease them?

- Have any of these habits of appeasing fear become an idol?

- How can I bring Jesus' love into the times I feel afraid?

Challenge Ten

This fear junk is going to take some hard work on your part to unlearn, but we can start with this simple challenge. Since, after answering the above questions, we have identified the habits we've created to manage our fear, we can add a highly beneficial item to our emotional to-do list. Whatever fears you are taking inventory of, be sure to keep an eye out for your responses to them.

- Does the fear make you withdraw, and hide away?

- Do you try to increasingly control situations where you encounter things that bring about fear?

No matter how you currently react to the presence of fear, know that we are going to change those response patterns for the better. Take a good look at the things you fear most. Are these rational fears, based in reality? Are they likely occurrences, or do they prey on moments of emotional weakness?

- Write down a comforting truth, preferably something scriptural, that directly counters the weight of the fear you're carrying (there are some examples below).

- Each time you confront a situation which causes that knot in your stomach or makes your heart race in panic, pull out that piece of truth and literally *hold onto it* as you recognize the authority Christ has over your life, and over the things you fear.

- Read the scripture or piece of truth to yourself, take a few deep breaths, and invite God into the moment of chaos. Invite him to join you in your boat, and believe that he wants to overcome the fear in you.

"Love will never invoke fear. Perfect love expels fear, particularly the fear of punishment. The one who fears punishment has not been completed through love."
1st John 4:18

"He is ever present with me; at all times He goes before me. I will not live in fear or abandon my calling because He stands at my right hand. " Psalm 16:8

"God is our shelter and our strength. When troubles seem near, God is nearer, and He is ready to help. So why run and hide? No fear no pacing, no biting fingernails. When the earth spins out of control, we are sure and fearless. When mountains crumble and the waters run wile, we are sure and fearless. Even in heavy winds and huge waves, or as mountains shake, we are sure and fearless. " Psalm 46:3

Let Us Pray

Lord, we come to you in desperation. We admit to you that our fear has taken control far too many times, and we declare that now is the time we want to live life unhindered by fear and its stupid lies. We surrender to you now our places of emotional weakness; the times we have panicked and misunderstood your heart towards us in our moments of overwhelming fear. We invite you into the places of our hearts that have been locked up by worry and ask that you break the chains and remove the locks for good. We ask that you teach us the difference between wise caution and flesh-driven fear, that we may have wisdom in how to react to situations that make us uneasy. We ask for the boldness to change the unhealthy habits surrounding our panic so that we can replace them with habits of reciting and embracing the truth: that you have overcome death, and every lesser thing, so that we can know peace. We ask that you fill our hearts with a certainty of who you are, the power you posses, and the authority you have given to us as your daughters and co-heirs with Christ. We believe that we can live in a way that embraces your truth and demolishes the grip that fear has on us. We want to live in a way that honors you, and demonstrates to others that we have full faith in you. Help us to embrace this reality as we seek to dethrone the idols of appeasing our fears, and restore you to your rightful place as the ruler of our hearts.

Calling Out to the Messes

Why don't we chat about your community for a moment?

Not your Facebook friends. Not your Instagram followers. I mean your real life, face to face, communion and fellowship with people in your circle. Think long and hard about your core people, here.

What do those relationships look like?
What kind of fruit do you see coming from them?
When you spend time with these men and women, do you feel encouraged?
Do you feel refreshed?
Do you feel challenged or convicted or inspired to do more for the Lord?

Maybe instead, you feel drained, or you feel jealous. You might even leave feeling like you need to be different, rather than to be a better version of yourself. Maybe you feel like you need to one-up them in some way.

I ask these questions in search of honest answers, because I honestly fear that our generation is missing the entire point of community. We have seamlessly traded real conversations for quip-filled Instagram posts. We have replaced the word "friend" with the result of a button you click on Facebook. We have taken good relationships and fed them to the wolves of comparison at the cost of true community. We are so obsessed with presenting ourselves as these well-put-together women that we no longer leave much time for vulnerability. Without that, I do not see how community will flourish in our lives. We have to get *real* if we ever hope to be really *close*.

I say all of this having lived much of my adult life without such community. If there is anything I have learned thus far, it is this: community does not typically occur by accident. It takes intentional efforts on the parts of everyone involved to create sustainable relationships. Life without genuine fellowship is a lonely one, and oh, how the enemy loves to pounce on our lonely moments like a lion going in for the kill.

So here is my encouragement; instead of sitting around, scrolling through your newsfeed and watching "everyone else" spend time with people they care about...get off your phone. Find someone you care about. Spend time with them. Get off your phone. Get off your phone. Get off your phone.

I truly believe social media has redefined our realm of understanding friendship, in some ways for the good, and in some ways for the bad. I say this having lived in the generation that actually experienced the creation and explosion of social media, I can honestly say I have lived through life before a cell phone and text messaging and periscope (I still don't know what that is, by the way) and lived to tell of the transition. It has been brutal and wonderful all at the same time.

In the spirit of transparency, we can admit that most of us have a love-hate relationship with our smart phone. In the midst of all of our connections, we are lonely, and we fear that we will always be alone. We have failed to find our people and stick with them because we are so busy posing our coffee mugs hoping to gain some approval from strangers on the internet. We love being able to share our best moments, but we hate to see everyone else's when we are left out of them.

It is okay to admit that we get jealous over dumb things like Instagram likes on a photo. It is okay to admit that we refresh our newsfeed every five seconds after we post something new because a part of us is looking, desperately, for validation from the number of likes on that photo of our puppy or baby or cup of coffee. However, it is *not* okay for us to go on like this. We cannot, and we will not, survive at the rate we are depending on social media to define our worth. We must impart more than the skill of a selfie to the women who will follow after us. *This* is where a great and encouraging and honest community of women can come in—to hold us accountable. They are the ones who struggle alongside us in this broken world, and can remind us to turn our phones off and look up to the beautiful world and women around us.

Don't get me wrong, I love social media. I am a frequent poster and blogger and status-updater, but it takes *balance*. I cannot post something online, only to stare at my phone for the next hour, desperately checking my "popularity" every five minutes. Those little hearts on Instagram aren't real love, y'all. Sure, our newsfeeds are full of likes and comments and texts and tweets, yet we still come up feeling empty...*because those things are empty*. They were never intended to fill us up. They are not the validation we were created to need. Maybe you are all stronger women than I, and have not struggled as I have, but chances are if you are over the age of I don't know, six, that you have been there, and you do struggle.

Do not struggle alone.
Do not struggle needlessly.
Do not struggle over dumb stuff.
...and if you do, do not struggle alone.

Community should spur us on to do great things for the Kingdom. Isn't that the original design we see in the scriptures? Where people gathered in the name of Jesus—radical, incredible things happened. That is what I want to see for us. That is what I want to experience. So, why don't we? Let's examine some of the things our modern day society tells us about community, and some of the pitfalls we can easily be trapped by in terms of Christian community.

First of all, community does not mean that you find your clones and stick with 'em. If everyone you surround yourself with believes exactly as you do and behaves in the same manner, you have missed the point of community. The goal is not about consistency; it is about cooperation as the body. If the people you hold dearest happen to have all of the same strengths and weaknesses as you, it is like having a body with seven arms and no legs. You have a lot of the same going on which does not exactly promote growth. Now, if you have friends with similar careers or life goals, I am not knocking that. I understand the importance of having "your people". What I am saying is this: your community should challenge your views and force you to examine what you believe. It is not about being in a Christian bubble. It is about taking the conceptual and making it practical. That is the heart of community—centered on fellowship, action, and compassion.

Secondly, community is not a competition. That goes directly against the heart of how we are supposed to treat each other as believers. For goodness sake, it says it plainly in the word. As much as it is up to you, live peaceably with all (wo)men. Our current view of community reminds me of the apostles, sitting around at the last supper. They are in the midst of Jesus' last hours on the earth before his trial and crucifixion, and do you know what they spend their time doing? They are arguing over who Jesus loves the most. *Seriously.* Twelve grown men are sitting around a dinner table with Jesus, as our world as we know it is about to change forever. They almost miss the significant things Jesus is saying because they are too busy worrying about who wore it best or who has the cutest blog or who really understood what Jesus was saying in all of those parables. Get the picture? How often do we miss the whispers of Jesus in our community because we are far too busy competing needlessly against each other? Her success does not constitute your failure, and vice versa. Repeat that as many times as you need to, because *real* community is about encouraging, uplifting, and celebrating one another in the little and big victories.

We have to ensure that our community is not based on a need for recognition or status. If that is what we are about, we are in the wrong movement. So I will say this—stop trying to run someone else's trail. You have been given yours, just as they have been given theirs. We are each walking our own path, not racing down the same one.

Thirdly, community is supposed to be a safe space that both cultivates vulnerability and encourages growth. They are your sounding board if you think God is leading you do something new. They are your prayer warriors when your heart is so weary, you run out of words. They are your intercessors to step into a place of prayer for you when the battle gets overwhelming. They are your partners in overcoming obstacles, there to cheer you on in the little and big victories. They are your reality check, meant to caution and exhort you when you've stepped out of line or started bowing down to an idol.

So, if this community stuff is so life-giving, why don't we see more of it? Why doesn't our culture seem to value this? Well, we have to look at that from a few different angles.

For one thing, we have a highly competitive culture. We are very much focused on the bottom line. Whether its family goals, career goals, ministry goals, or a combination of all of the above—it leaves little room for vulnerability and openly admitting our weaknesses. I mean, who really enjoys talking about their flaws, failures, and sin? That kind of conversation does not come naturally. Our flesh, at the urging and shaping of our culture, prides itself on strength and independence. Can you see how that doesn't really mesh too well with the biblical views on community? Again, here we are, needing to change our thoughts so that we can act in a way conducive to honest community.

Additionally, community takes a serious time investment—and

it is not the kind of investment we get a direct, immediate, and tangible return on. In our instant-gratification seeking culture, community seems backwards. In a world of professional networks meant to accelerate our careers, community says to slow down and invest in another person's wellbeing. This is backwards to the culture we live in. As I said, community rarely happens on accident.

Finally, we have to look at it from a time-invested stand point. We are all masters of our own busy schedules. We plan and plan and fill in the empty spaces on our planners because an entire afternoon without something to do just seems, well, wasteful. Doesn't it? We are hard wired to manage our time well as young women. We have to jam pack every hour of every day to get ahead. To be the best. To feel important. I mean, really. If we are not busy, do we still matter? It is a lot of bad thinking to unpack, but if we push through, we will get to find our people, and stick with 'em in the good times and bad.

We see quite a bit of talk about this idea of gathering together in the New Testament. There are a lot of ideas about it, instructions on how to do it, and encouragements to share with each other when you meet up. Assembling together as a like-minded group of believers is nothing new, but I believe that now more than ever, a tight-knit Christian community makes a bold statement about our faith. It is so incredibly different from what our society mandates that we do with our time, that it surely makes an impact on others when they see us, selflessly loving one another in hopes of gaining nothing but an increased knowledge of who Jesus is and how He loves through us. People will want to know a Jesus that makes people love each other the way we should when we gather together. This applies whether it be church on a Sunday morning, or at a coffee shop on a Friday night. Community should invite others in—not remain shut off and reserved for an exclusive few.

I will encourage you to step out in a time of seeking community.

This is for you, introverts or anxiety sufferers or those of you simply trying to breathe under the weight of depression and grief and the hard seasons of life. Do not fall into the trap of thinking you need to be, or deserve to be, alone. That is a lie and we need to call it like we see it to move on. I know. I truly and deeply know how much easier it is to withdraw. To retreat. To sit alone in your hurt and let it hurt. There is a time for that. Jesus Himself withdrew at different, often pivotal moments, in the New Testament. We need the balance of rest and engagement, but we cannot simply sit at home in our sweatpants and wait for friends to find us. Invite people over to sit in sweatpants with you, then have some good conversation while you're at it.

It does not have to be a formal Church-coordinated event. It does not have to be a big group of women with perfect hair and really nice houses. It can just be women in your life that take the time to see in person. To get some good face-to-face time in. Make it a commitment. Agree that you will go when anxiety strikes and when tears are on their way. Agree to go even when you absolutely do not feel like it—because that is when we most need the community.

You do not have to share all of your mess at once or show up like a basket case, unless you are really in a place where you need to just show up at a friend's house a cry for an hour or so. Then, do that. My point is, do not disengage from the world around you when you are hurting or searching or uncertain. If we wait until our lives are settled or slowed down or good enough to join in the fellowship of community, we never will.

There won't ever be a time where this kind of community is fully convenient for us, but that in no way negates its necessity.

Case and point. I hate hate hate, one more time, hate meeting new people when I'm in a season of writing—in other words, "unemployed" in the traditional sense of the word. My pride rears its ugly head and I literally dread the imminent question,

"So Chelsey, what do you do?" Part of me likes the good ol', "I'm prepping for law school" answer. I mean, I bought the LSAT book and visited a few schools, so there is some validity there. Kind of.

The honest translation? *"Well, super successful lady who I just met with flawless nails and perfect hair, I quit my day job to write a book that I don't have a publisher for. I spend my days pacing around my apartment trying to think of whit-filled things to post to my blog that my mom reads, and sometimes I pretend to do yoga, but just long enough to validate posting a photo to Instagram."*

Yeah. You think the law school answer sounds better, too? I thought so.

All of that to say, you're not the only one who would rather shy away from community when life seems unglamorous, and you are not alone in the awkward search for your people. It might take you some time to find them, but once you do, hold on to them. Pour into those friendships. Treat them the way you would want a best friend to treat you. Encourage them. Pray for them. Better yet, pray with them. Soak in the idea that your people, if they are worth their salt, will be there for you on the days you do not feel like talking but need to talk and want to cry but do not want to leave the house and just need a hug and a good chai latte. Trust that they will be there for those days, and return the favor when the time comes.

I am not entirely sure why making friends has become so much more difficult the farther along we get into adulthood, but it truly has. Maybe we feel some skewed sense of obligation to take ourselves seriously, but I am still all for late night PJ parties where we talk about our feelings and each too much popcorn. Maybe you need to be the one that initiates this kind of community if you do not see it happening in your proximity. Maybe you need to be the one who sends that awkward first, "Hey, let's grab coffee this week!" text message and trust that it will grow into something deeper. Every community has to start somewhere.

Why not here?

Alright, so, I am emphasizing this community thing pretty firmly. I will cautiously remind you that it cannot define you, but it can certainly affirm the identity you have been given in Christ. These are your people who will remind you who you really are during your quarter life crises and job searches and all the days you tell God you just need to move overseas to love on orphans. Anyone else have those days?

My hope is that we have established the importance of community, but please hear this friend: it is not important because this book you picked up says it is. It is important because Jesus calls us to live in tight-knit fellowship with the people around us. It is not a mere suggestion—it is a scriptural mandate. Sorry, ladies. Friends are apparently not optional. We have to let others into our messy lives, and do so bravely.

In a world of filters, we have to be the open windows. Transparent. Curtains drawn. Let the light in.

I still think of some of my dear friends during what I now come to recognize as the one of most difficult seasons in my life. I had just returned from a few months in Southern Africa and was reeling with emotion about being "home". I wanted to pack my bags and go immediately back to life overseas, and God said a big fat "no". I then had to drop out of my last semester of college due to a clerical error. I was in a job where I was treated poorly. I got engaged to the man of my dreams in the same month my parents announced their divorce. Bottom line? It was a confusing time and I wanted desperately to retreat and hide myself away. It seemed easier to sit in my sweats and wish for a better scenario than to confront the reality of my circumstance.

It was during this time that the friends I held so dearly all chimed in. They told me I was intelligent, when I worried about my academic status. They reminded me I was called, equipped, and capable when my job made me feel incompetent. They spoke the truth over me that the Lord was at work in my life, even in the crappiest of days. Perhaps most importantly, they encouraged me to get help and show grace to myself in the process.

I am still moved when I think about the beauty and boldness of their honesty with me in the rainy seasons. That is exactly what "your people" are supposed to do. These are the people who are not afraid to speak truth into our darkest moments. Did the things they had to say define me? No. Not by any means. Their encouraging and truthful words reminded me of who I am in Christ. They were daily proof to me that I had an incredible support system; my tangible reminders that I did not walk alone. They encouraged me to remember that God is at work in the whispers of pain and confusion. They reminded be that there is a bigger picture. That is what community is for, truly. I pray that you find people like that, who will call you on your junk and love you while work through it.

There is one, last essential aspect of community, that I feel we have missed. Yes, communities are there to encourage and uplift but *not simply for encouragements' sake.* I tell you in earnest, if your community does not spend any time discussing sin or struggles or call you out on your crap—you are not in a real community, you are in an adult play date group.

The purpose of community is not to pad your ego, but rather to call you out when your pride rears its head. Your community is there to show you grace, yes, but not to comfort you in your sin. That is what grace does. It draws us out of sin. It makes it so that we are not afraid to face Jesus when we repent. Our communities should embody this above all else, and if they do not, we need to reexamine our reasons for participating in community to begin with.

In practicality, a real friend will tell you what you need to hear-- even if it makes you want to punch them in the face. Recently, there was a time I was a hormonal vomit machine at the hands of my morning sickness. I was cranky, lazy, and downright selfish in my attitude. When confessing this to a dear friend, as real friendships make space for these things, I sent a lengthy message detailing the situation. You know, the kind where your iPhone can only show a preview of the text because it's so dang long.

While my flesh was hoping she would justify my selfish behavior, my spirit was desperately needing admonishment. And you know what? She *corrected* me. And she did not care one bit if it made me mad. She did not care if my flesh was offended. She spoke what my spirit needed to hear, and that, friends, is the *perfect* definition of community—they say what needs to be said, even when it makes you want to punch them in the face. They are not afraid to step on your toes for the sake of your relationship with Christ. They want you to grow, even if it costs them a few difficult conversations.

These are the types of relationships I pray we can learn to have. These are the people you need to find, appreciate, and hold on to even when it is awkward or inconvenient or ruffles your feathers. I believe this is what Jesus intends for us to have as believers—not just a group of people we sit with on Sundays, but people we can go to the other six days of the week with our sins and problems and confusions and tears and messes. Especially in this season of unlearning, *these* are the type of people you need if you want accountability in doing the hard things, like reclaiming the daring truth of biblical femininity.

"Let us consider how to inspire each other to greater love and to righteous deeds, not forgetting to gather as a community, as some have forgotten, but encouraging each other, especially as the day *of His return* approaches."

Hebrews 10:24-25

"For in the same way that one body has so many different parts, each with different functions; we, too—the many—are different parts that form one body in the Anointed One. Each one of us is joined with one another, *and we become together what we could not be alone."* Romans 12:4-5

"Make every effort to preserve the unity the Spirit has already created, with peace binding you together." Ephesians 4:3

"The community continually committed themselves to learning what the apostles taught them, gathering for fellowship, breaking bread, and praying. Everyone felt a sense of awe because the apostles were doing many signs and wonders among them There was an intense sense of togetherness among all who believed; they shared all their material possessions in trust. They sold and possessions and goods that did not benefit the community and used the money to help everyone in need. They were unified as they worshiped at the temple day after day. In homes, they broke bread and shared meals with glad and generous hearts. The new disciples praised God, and they enjoyed the goodwill of all the people of the city. Day after day the Lord added to their number everyone who was experiencing liberation." Acts 2:42-47

Questions for Unlearning

- What kind of community do I have in my life?

- Is there any accountability provided by this community, or do we enable each other to continue in sin?

- Who, in my life right now, would be willing to call me on my junk if I started to lose perspective?

- Who, in my life right now, would I be willing to call out in the same way?
- If I don't see this kind of fruitful community around me, what steps can I take *today* to get one started?

- How can I boldly invite others into my life in an authentic way that encourages mutual vulnerability?

Final Challenge

My final challenge to you is this: find your people, and unlearn *with* them. Do not attempt to figure all of this out on your own, got it? Surely, there are pieces of your story you may prefer to work on with the Lord, and only Him. However, there are also pieces of your story, even the not-so-pretty parts, that will serve as an encouragement and testament of God's faithfulness to the women around you. Do not be afraid to share in the muddled process; to do so bravely, in a messy-bun-sans-makeup kind of way. If we hope to radically challenge the women around us to live a life unashamed of the things they have had to unlearn, it is up to us to first set the example, and to then pave the way for brave authenticity in a culture that is far too busy chasing perfection.

This is your journey, and I pray you are not afraid to invite others into it.
This is the time to question, together, the things you have been taught to accept at face value from a broken world.
This is our season to be refreshed in truth, and covered in grace.
May we live it out fiercely, with a desperate dependence on the God who made us to look, think, and act differently than what we see around us.

The unlearned adventure is just beginning, friend.
Let's get to work, together.

About the Author

Chelsey is a Christ-follower, wife + mother, author, and encourager. She spends her days writing with The UNEDITED Movement and drinking too much coffee. Her passion is for making Christ known and reminding women to embrace their mess while letting Jesus love them out of it. She currently resides in Northern Virginia with her husband, Taylor, newborn son, Benaiah, and rescue pup, Hank Williams.

To give feedback + join in the conversation please contact the author via the following:

www.chelseylynnemead.com
www.instagram.com/chelsmead
chelsey.l.mead@gmail.com